What Should
Economists Do?

James M. Buchanan is the Holbert L. Harris University Professor and the General Director of the Center for Study of Public Choice at George Mason University. His distinguished teaching career has included positions at the University of Tennessee, Florida State University, the University of Virginia, and Virginia Polytechnic Institute and State University. His many books include *The Calculus of Consent* (1962) with Gordon Tullock, *Cost and Choice* (1969), *The Limits of Liberty* (1975), and *The Reason of Rules* (1985) with Geoffrey Brennan. He has been president of the Mont Pèlerin Society, the Western Economics Association, and the Southern Economic Association. In 1986 he received the Nobel Prize in Economics.

What Should Economists Do?

James M. Buchanan

Preface by
H. Geoffrey Brennan and
Robert D. Tollison

Liberty Fund

This book is published by Liberty Fund, Inc., a foundation established to
encourage study of the ideal of a society of free and responsible individuals.

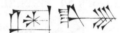

The cuneiform inscription that serves as our logo and as a design element for
Liberty Fund books is the earliest-known written appearance of the word
"freedom" *(amagi),* or "liberty." It is taken from a clay document written about
2300 B.C. in the Sumerian city-state of Lagash.

4th printing (2023)

Library of Congress Cataloging in Publication Data

Buchanan, James M.
  What should economists do?

  Includes bibliographical references and index.
  1. Economics. 2. Economics-Methodology.
I. Title.
HB71.B78   330   79-19511
ISBN 0-913966-64-9 (hardcover edition)
ISBN 0-913966-65-7 (paperback edition)

Liberty Fund, Inc.
11301 North Meridian Street
Carmel, Indiana 46032
libertyfund.org

Contents

Preface

This collection of essays was gathered for two purposes. First, and most importantly, it provides relatively easy access to a group of significant papers on methodology in economics, written by a man whose work has spawned a methodological revolution in the way economists and other scholars think about government and governmental activity. Second, it provides a means to honor a distinguished colleague at a stage in his career when such tributes are deemed appropriate.

The significance of James Buchanan's contributions to economics is undeniable. As a founder of the burgeoning subdiscipline of public choice, as a moral and legal philosopher, as a welfare economist who has consistently and at times almost singlehandedly defended the primacy of the contractarian ethic, and as a public finance theorist and father of a modern school of public finance, Buchanan's work has had worldwide recognition, and it is not too much to expect that in the years ahead his influence will significantly change the face and direction of modern economics. Underlying all these aspects of his work there has been a consistent set of beliefs about the nature of economics, about the appropriate subject matter of the discipline, and about the appropriate method for dealing with that subject matter.

To bring together Buchanan's important essays on method, many of which have not previously been published, therefore seemed to us an important and worthwhile task. The resulting collection provides not only an insight for understanding the work of an important scholar, but also a blueprint for vigorous and significant scholarship by others.

The papers themselves and the occasion for their publication are self-explanatory and require no comment. There are, however, two points that should be made about the volume. First, the selection of essays and their organization primarily reflect our judgment and not Buchanan's. We prevailed on him to provide the brief postscript essay, but in all other respects he was simply an innocent bystander. He cleared the papers that we chose and gave them a quick tidying-up, but he did not select, organize, and edit them in the way he might have done had he been producing the book entirely under his own aegis. For this reason any criticisms of selection and organization should be directed to us, not at the author.

Second, this book is meant to honor James Buchanan's vigorous ongoing academic life. Since important ideas continue to flow at an unabated rate from Buchanan's work, it is much too early to talk of his legacy to scholarship, and we do not attempt to do so here. One thing, however, is clear. A significant dimension of that legacy does not, and will not, lie on paper, but rather in the minds and spirits of his students. More than most teachers, Buchanan has been able to scatter around the universities and research centers of the world, men and women who bear identifiably the marks of their intellectual heritage—creative thinking, a concern with ideas rather than tools, and a passion for hard work and academic integrity. We join with those students in dedicating this book to Buchanan because, like this book, they are the fruit of his own hands.

H. GEOFFREY BRENNAN
ROBERT D. TOLLISON

Blacksburg, Virginia
October 1979

What Should Economists Do?

Part One

Scope and Method

1

What Should Economists Do?

> But it is not the popular movement, but the traveling of the minds of men who sit in the seat of Adam Smith that is really serious and worthy of all attention.
>
> LORD ACTON, *Letters of Lord Acton to Mary Gladstone,*
>   ed. Herbert Paul (London: George Allen, 1904), p. 212

I propose to examine the "traveling of the minds of men who sit in the seat of Adam Smith," those who try to remain within the "strict domain of science," and to ask the following questions: What are economists doing? What "should" they be doing? In these efforts to heed the counsel of Lord Acton, I proceed squarely against the advice of a modern economist whose opinions I regard with respect, George Stigler. He tells us that it is folly to become concerned with methodology before the age of sixty-five. As a value statement, Stigler's admonition can hardly be discussed. But, as a hypothesis, it can be refuted, at least by analogy with an ordinary roadmap. I remain notorious for my failure to look quickly enough at highway-route maps,

This chapter was initially presented as the Presidential Address to the Southern Economic Association at its annual meeting in November 1963. It was subsequently published in *Southern Economic Journal* 30 (January 1964): 213–22. Permission to reprint the paper in this volume is gratefully acknowledged.

hoping always that some intuitive directional instinct will keep me along the planned pattern of my journey. I learned many years ago that "optimal" behavior involves stopping soon after one gets "lost," after uncertainty beyond a certain limit is reached, and consulting a properly drawn map. The analogy with scientific methodology seems to be a close one. Unless we can, for some reason, accept the ever-changing activities of economists as being always a part of the necessary evolution of the discipline through time, as being "on the highway," it is essential that we look occasionally at the map or model for scientific progress that each of us surely carries around, consciously or unconsciously, in his head.

By proposing to examine critically what economists do I am also, you will note, rejecting the familiar proposition advanced by Jacob Viner that "economics is what economists do," a proposition that Frank Knight converted into full circle when he added that "economists are those who do economics." This functional definition of our discipline begs the very question that I want to raise, if not to answer here. Economists should, I think, face up to their basic responsibility; they should at least try to know their subject matter.

Let me call your attention to a much-neglected principle enunciated by Adam Smith. In chapter two of *The Wealth of Nations* he states that the principle which gives rise to the division of labor, from which so many advantages are derived, "is not originally the effects of any human wisdom, which foresees and intends that general opulence to which it gives occasion. It is the necessary, though very slow and gradual, consequence of a certain propensity in human nature which has in view no such extensive utility; the propensity to truck, barter, and exchange one thing for another." Somewhat surprisingly, it seems to me, the relevance and the significance of this "propensity to truck, barter, and exchange" have been overlooked in most of the exegetical treatments of Smith's work. But surely here is his answer to what economics or political economy is all about.

Economists "should" concentrate their attention on a particular form of human activity, and upon the various institutional arrangements that arise as a result of this form of activity. Man's behavior in the market relationship, reflecting the propensity to truck and to barter, and the manifold variations in structure that this relationship can take—these are the proper subjects for the economist's study. In saying this, I am, of course, making a value statement that you may or may not support. Consider this paper, if you will, as an "essay in persuasion."

The elementary and basic approach that I suggest places "the theory of markets" and not the "theory of resource allocation" at center stage. My plea is really for the adoption of a sophisticated "catallactics," an approach to our discipline that has been advanced earlier, much earlier, by Archbishop Whately and the Dublin school, by H. D. Macleod, by the American Arthur Latham Perry, by Alfred Ammon and still others.[1] It is not my purpose here, and it is not within my competence, to review the reasons for the failures of these men to convince their colleagues and their descendants. I note only that the view that they advanced,

---

[1] For a review of this approach in terms of the doctrinal history, see Israel Kirzner, *The Economic Point of View* (New York: D. Van Nostrand, 1960), chap. 4. This book provides a good summary of the various approaches to the "economic point of view."

and one that has never been wholly absent from the main-stream of thinking,[2] is perhaps more in need of stress now than during the times in which they worked.

In a brief treatment it is helpful to make bold charges against ideas or positions taken by leading figures. In this respect I propose to take on Lord Robbins as an adversary and to state, categorically, that his all too persuasive de-lineation of our subject field has served to retard, rather than to advance, scientific progress. You are, of course, all familiar with the Robbins statement of the definition of the economic problem, the one that has found its way into almost all of our textbooks. The economic problem involves the allocation of scarce means among alternative or com-peting ends. The problem is one of *allocation*, made neces-sary by the fact of *scarcity*, the necessity to *choose*. Only since *The Nature and Significance of Economic Science*[3] have economists so exclusively devoted their energies to the problems raised by scarcity, broadly considered, and to the necessity for the making of allocative decisions.

In Robbins' vision, our subject field is a problem or set of problems, not a characteristic form of human activity. We were better off, methodologically speaking, in the less definitive Marshallian world when economists did in fact study man in his ordinary business of making a living. In his attempt to remain wholly neutral as to ends, Robbins left economics open-ended, so to speak. Search him as you will, and you will not find an explicit statement as to *whose*

---

[2] For a recent paper in which the exchange basis for economic analysis is plainly accepted, see Kenneth E. Boulding, "Toward a Pure Theory of Threat Systems," *American Economic Review* (May 1963): 424–34; esp. 424–26.

[3] London: Macmillan, 1932.

ends are alternatives. His neutrality extends to the point of remaining wholly silent on the identity of the choosing agent, and few economists seem to have bothered with the difficult issue of identifying properly the entity for whom the defined economic problem exists. It is thus by quite natural or normal extension that the economic problem moves from that one which is confronted by the individual person to that facing the larger family group, the business firm, the trade union, the trade association, the church, the local community, the regional or state government, the national government, and, finally, the world.[4]

To illustrate the confusion that this lack of identification introduces, let me mention my most respected of all professors, Frank Knight, who has taught us all to think in terms of the five functions of "an economic system," presumably, "any economic system." In the Knightian introduction to our subject we talk about the "social organization" that performs these five familiar "social" functions. For whom? This is the question to which I return. Presumably, the answer is for the whole of the relevant collective group, for society. To be somewhat more explicit, let me cite Milton Friedman, who says, if I remember his classroom introduction correctly, "economics is the study of how a particular society solves its economic problem."

Knight and Friedman are good examples for my pur-

---

[4] In his presidential address to the American Economic Association, delivered in 1949, Howard S. Ellis criticized the arbitrariness with which ends may be selected under the Robbins definition. Ellis's whole approach has much in common with that taken in this paper. In my view, however, Ellis, through his overemphasis on the "choice" aspects of economics, failed to make his critique of Robbins as effective as it might have been. See Howard S. Ellis, "The Economic Way of Thinking," *American Economic Review* (March 1950): 1–12.

poses, since both of these men, despite their own differences on many particulars of economic policy, are men with whom, broadly and generally, I agree on principles of political-philosophical order. In their introductions to economics, both of these men seem to identify "society" as the entity that confronts the economic problem about which we, as professional economists, should be concerned, the entity, presumably, whose ends are to count in the appropriate calculus of margins. If they should be explicitly questioned, I am sure that both Knight and Friedman, and Robbins as well, would say that "society," as such, must always be conceived in terms of its individual members. Hence, when reference is made to a particular society solving its economic problem, this is really only shorthand for saying "a particular group of individuals who have organized themselves socially solving their economic problem."

The important point is, however, that we do, in ordinary and everyday usage, require a supplementary or an additional step in our basic definitional process before we break down the societal language into its meaningful individual components. This amounts to locking the barn door without being sure that we have ever had or will have a horse inside. Somewhat more technically, this procedure assumes that there is meaningful content in economics for "social welfare"; it prejudges the central issue that has been debated in theoretical welfare economics, and comes down squarely with the utilitarians. This seems to be a clear case where the basic conceptual apparatus has not yet been brought into line with modern developments. But this conceptual apparatus is extremely important, especially when most practitioners are too busy to bother with methodology. The definition of our subject makes it all too easy to slip across the bridge between personal or individual units of decision and "social" aggregates. In principle, this bridge is most difficult to cross, as most economists fully recognize when put to it. And, in one sense, my whole plea here is summarized by saying to economists, "get back or stay on the side of the bridge where you belong."

The utilitarians tried to cross the bridge by summing utilities. Robbins quite properly told them to cease and desist. But in remaining what I have called "open-ended," in emphasizing the universality of the allocation problem without at the same time defining the identity of the choosing agent, Robbins' contribution to method has tended to promote a proliferation of the very confusion that he had hoped to prevent. Economists, paying heed to Robbins, now know when they cross the bridge; they explicitly state their own value judgments in the form of "social welfare functions." Once having done this, they feel free to maximize to their own hearts' content. And they do so within the bounds of methodological propriety, à la Robbins. They have, of course, abandoned his neutrality-of-ends position, but they have been straightforward about this. And, by the very fact of this neutrality, their explicitly stated personal version of "social" value is as acceptable as any other. They continue to work on an *economic* problem, as such, and this problem appears superficially to be the one that is generally referred to in the definitional introduction to our subject. These "social" economists are wholly concerned with the allocation of scarce resources among competing ends or uses.

I submit that theirs is not legitimate activity for practitioners in economics, as I want to define the discipline. In hastening to explain my heresy, I should emphasize that my argument is not centered on whether or not economists explicitly introduce value judgments into their work. This important issue is a wholly different one from that which I am trying to advance here. I want economists to quit concerning themselves with allocation problems *per se,* with *the problem,* as it has been traditionally defined. The vocabulary of science is important here, and as T. D. Weldon once suggested, the very word *problem* in and of itself implies the presence of "solution." Once the format has been established in allocation terms, some solution is more or less automatically suggested. Our whole study becomes one of applied maximization of a relatively simple computational sort. Once the ends to be maximized are provided by the social welfare function, everything becomes computational, as my colleague, Rutledge Vining, has properly noted. If there is really nothing more to economics than this, we had as well turn it all over to the applied mathematicians. This does, in fact, seem to be the direction in which we are moving, professionally, and developments of note, or notoriety, during the past two decades consist largely of improvements in what are essentially computing techniques, in the mathematics of social engineering. What I am saying is that we should keep these contributions in perspective; I am urging that they be recognized for what they are, contributions to applied mathematics, to managerial science if you will, but not to our chosen subject field, which we, for better or for worse, call "economics."

Let me illustrate with reference to the familiar distinction, or presumed distinction, between an economic and a technological problem. What is the sophomore, who has completed his "principles," expected to reply to the question: What is the difference between an economic and a technological problem? He might respond something like the following: "An economic problem arises when mutually conflicting ends are present, when choices must be made among them. A technological problem, by comparison, is characterized by the fact that there is only one end to be maximized. There is a single best or optimal solution." We conclude that the sophomore has read the standard textbooks. We then proceed to ask that he give us practical examples. He might then say: "The consumer finds that she has only $10 to spend in the supermarket; she confronts an economic problem in choosing among the many competing products that are available for meeting diverse ends and objectives. By contrast, the construction engineer has $1,000,000 allotted to build a dam to certain specifications. There is only one best way to do this; locating this way constitutes the technological problem." Most of us would, I suspect, be inclined to give this student good grades for such answers until another, erratic and eccentric, student on the back row says: "But there is really no difference."

I need not continue the illustration in detail. In the context of my earlier remarks, it seems clear that the second student has the proper answer, and that the orthodox textbook reply is wrong. Surely any difference between what we normally call the economic problem and what we call the technological problem is one of degree only, of the degree to which the function to be maximized is specified in advance of the choices to be made.

In one sense, the theory of choice presents a paradox. If the utility function of the choosing agent is fully defined in advance, choice becomes purely mechanical. No "decision," as such, is required; there is no weighing of alternatives. On the other hand, if the utility function is not wholly defined, choice becomes real, and decisions become unpredictable mental events. If I know what I want, a computer can make all of my choices for me. If I do not know what I want, no possible computer can derive my utility function since it does not really exist. But the distinction to be drawn here is surely that about the knowledge of the utility function. The difference is analogous to driving on a clear and a foggy highway. It is not that between economics and technology. Neither the consumer in the supermarket nor the construction engineer faces an economic problem; both face essentially technological problems.

The theory of choice must be removed from its position of eminence in the economist's thought processes. The theory of choice, of resource allocation, call it what you will, assumes no special role for the economist, as opposed to any other scientist who examines human behavior. Lest you become overly concerned, let me hasten to say that most, if not all, of what now passes muster in the theory of choice will remain even in my ideal manual of instructions. I should emphasize that what I am suggesting is not so much a change in the basic content of what we study as a change in the way we approach our material. I want economists to modify their thought processes, to look at the same phenomena through "another window," to use Nietzsche's appropriate metaphor. I want them to concentrate on *exchange* rather than on *choice*.

The very word *economics,* in and of itself, is partially responsible for some of the intellectual confusion. The "economizing" process leads us to think directly in terms of the theory of choice. I think it was Irving Babbitt who said that revolutions begin in dictionaries. Should I have my say, I should propose that we cease, forthwith, to talk about *economics* or *political economy*, although the latter is the much superior term. Were it possible to wipe the slate clean, I should recommend that we take up a wholly different term such as *catallactics,* or *symbiotics.* The second of these would, on balance, be preferred. Symbiotics is defined as the study of the association between dissimilar organisms, and the connotation of the term is that the association is mutually beneficial to all parties. This conveys, more or less precisely, the idea that should be central to our discipline. It draws attention to a unique sort of relationship, that which involves the cooperative association of individuals, one with another, even when individual interests are different. It concentrates on Adam Smith's "invisible hand," which so few noneconomists properly understand. As suggested above, important elements of the theory of choice remain in symbiotics. On the other hand, certain choice situations that are confronted by human beings remain wholly outside the symbiotic frame of reference. Robinson Crusoe, on his island before Friday arrives, makes decisions; his is the economic problem in the sense traditionally defined. This choice situation is not, however, an appropriate starting point for our discipline, even at the broadest conceptual level, as Whately correctly noted more than a century ago.[5] Crusoe's problem is, as I have said, essentially a computational one, and all that he need do to solve it is to program the built-in computer that he has in his mind. The uniquely symbiotic aspects of behavior, of human choice, arise only when Friday steps on

---

[5] Richard Whately, *Introductory Lectures on Political Economy* (London: B. Fellowes, 1831), p. 7. The same point is made by Arthur Latham Perry, *Elements of Political Economy* (New York: Charles Scribner, 1868), p. 27.

the island, and Crusoe is forced into *association* with another human being. The fact of association requires that a wholly different, and wholly new, sort of behavior take place, that of exchange, trade, or agreement. Crusoe may, of course, fail to recognize this new fact. He may treat Friday simply as a means to his own ends, as a part of nature, so to speak. If he does so, a fight ensues, and to the victor go the spoils. Symbiotics does not include the strategic choices that are present in such situations of pure conflict. On the other extreme, it does not include the choices that are involved in purely "integrative" systems, where the separate individual participants desire identical results.[6]

Crusoe, if he chooses to avoid pure conflict, and if he realizes that Friday's interests are likely to be different from his own, will recognize that mutual gains can be secured through cooperative endeavor, that is, through exchange or trade. This mutuality of advantage that may be secured by different organisms as a result of cooperative arrangements, be these simple or complex, is the one important truth in our discipline. There is no comparable principle, and the important place that has been traditionally assigned to the maximization norm that is called the "economic principle" reflects misguided emphasis.

Almost at the other extreme from the Crusoe models, the refinements in the theoretical model of perfectly competitive general equilibrium have been equally, if not more, productive of intellectual muddle. By imposing the condition that no participant in the economic process can independently influence the outcome of this process, all "social" content is squeezed out of individual behavior in market

---

[6] Boulding, *op. cit.*, distinguishes threat systems, exchange systems, and integrative systems of social order.

organization. The individual responds to a set of externally determined, exogenous variables, and his choice problem again becomes purely mechanical. The basic flaw in this model of perfect competition is not its lack of correspondence with observed reality; no model of predictive value exhibits this. Its flaw lies in its conversion of individual choice behavior from a social-institutional context to a physical-computational one. Given the "rules of the market," the perfectly competitive model yields a unique "optimum" or "equilibrium," a single point on the Paretian welfare surface. But surely this is nonsensical social science, and the institutionalist critics have been broadly on target in some of their attacks. Frank Knight has consistently stressed that, in perfect competition, there is no competition. He is, of course, correct, but, and for the same reason, there is no "trade" as such.

A market is not competitive by assumption or by construction. A market *becomes* competitive, and competitive rules *come to be* established as institutions emerge to place limits on individual behavior patterns. It is this *becoming* process, brought about by the continuous pressure of human behavior in exchange, that is the central part of our discipline, if we have one, not the dry rot of postulated perfection. A solution to a general-equilibrium set of equations is not predetermined by exogenously determined rules. A general solution, if there is one, *emerges* as a result of a whole network of evolving exchanges, bargains, trades, side payments, agreements, contracts which, finally at some point, ceases to renew itself. At each stage in this evolution toward solution there are *gains* to be made, there are exchanges possible, and this being true, the direction of movement is modified.

It is for these reasons that the model of perfect competition is of such limited explanatory value except when changes in variables exogenous to the system are introduced. There is no place in the structure of the model for internal change, change that is brought about by the men who continue to be haunted by the Smithean propensity. But surely the dynamic element in the economic system is precisely this continual evolution of the exchange process, as Schumpeter recognized in his treatment of entrepreneurial function.

How should the economist conceive the market organization? This is a central question, and the relevance of the difference in approach that I am emphasizing is directly shown by the two sharply conflicting answers. If the classical and currently renewed emphasis on the "wealth of nations" remains paramount, and if the logic of choice or allocation constitutes the "problem" element, the economist will look on market order as a *means* of accomplishing the basic economic functions that must be carried out in any society. The "market" becomes an engineered construction, a "mechanism," an "analogue calculating machine,"[7] a "computational device,"[8] one that processes information, accepts inputs, and transforms these into outputs which it then distributes. In this conception, the market, as a mechanism, is appropriately compared with government, as an alternative mechanism for accomplishing similar tasks. The second answer to the question is wholly different, although subtly so, and it is this second conception that I am trying to stress in this paper. The

[7] Paul A. Samuelson, "The Pure Theory of Public Expenditure," *Review of Economics and Statistics* (November 1954): 388.

[8] Takashi Negishi, "The Stability of a Competitive Economy: A Survey Article," *Econometrica* (October 1962): 639.

market or market organization is not a *means* toward the accomplishment of anything. It is, instead, the institutional embodiment of the voluntary exchange processes that are entered into by individuals in their several capacities. This is all that there is to it. Individuals are observed to co-operate with one another, to reach agreements, to trade. The network of relationships that emerges or evolves out of this trading process, the institutional framework, is called "the market." It is a setting, an arena, in which we, as econ-omists, as theorists (as onlookers), observe men attempt-ing to accomplish their own purposes, whatever these may be. And it is about these attempts that our basic theory is exclusively concerned if we would only recognize it as such. The boundaries are set by the limits of such cooperative endeavor; unilateral action is not part of the behavior pat-tern within our purview. In this conception, there is no explicit meaning of the term *efficiency* as applied to ag-gregative or composite results. It is contradictory to talk of the market as achieving "national goals," efficiently or inefficiently.

This does not imply that efficiency considerations are wholly eliminated in the conception that I am proposing. In fact, the opposite is true. The motivation for individuals to engage in trade, the source of the propensity, is surely that of "efficiency," defined in the personal sense of mov-ing from less preferred to more preferred positions, and doing so under mutually acceptable terms. An "inefficient" institution, one that produces largely "inefficient" results, cannot, by the nature of man, survive until and unless coer-cion is introduced to prevent the emergence of alternative arrangements.

Let me illustrate this point and, at the same time, indi-

cate the extension of the approach I am suggesting by re-
ferring to a familiar and simple example. Suppose that the
local swamp requires draining to eliminate or reduce mosquito breeding. Let us postulate that no single citizen in
the community has sufficient incentive to finance the full
costs of this essentially indivisible operation. Defined in the
orthodox, narrow way, the "market" fails; bilateral behavior of buyers and sellers does not remove the nuisance.
"Inefficiency" presumably results. This is, however, surely
an overly restricted conception of market behavior. If the
market institutions, defined so narrowly, will not work,
they will not meet individual objectives. Individual citizens
will be led, because of the same propensity, to search voluntarily for more inclusive trading or exchange arrangements.
A more complex institution may emerge to drain the swamp.
The task of the economist includes the study of all such
cooperative trading arrangements which become merely extensions of markets as more restrictively defined.

I have not got out of all the difficulties yet, however. You
may ask: Will it really be to the interest of any single citizen to contribute to the voluntary program of mosquito control? How is the "free rider" problem to be handled? This
specter of the free rider, found in many shapes and forms
in the literature of modern public finance theory, must be
carefully examined. In the first place, there has been some
confusion between total and marginal effects here. If a
pretty woman strolls through the hotel lobby, many tired
convention delegates may get some external benefits, but,
presumably, she finds it to her own advantage to stroll,
and few delegates would pay her to stroll more than she
already does. Nevertheless, to return to the swamp, there
may be cases where the expected benefits from draining are

not sufficiently high to warrant the emergence of some voluntary cooperative arrangement. And, in addition, the known or predicted presence of free riders may inhibit the cooperation of individuals who would otherwise contribute. In such situations, voluntary cooperation may never produce an "efficient" outcome for the individual members of the group. Hence, the "market," even in its most extended sense, may be said to "fail." What recourse is left to the individual in this case? It is surely that of transferring, again voluntarily, at least at some ultimate constitutional level, activities of the swamp-clearing sort to the community as a collective unit, with decisions delegated to specifically designated rules for making choices, and these decisions coercively enforced once they are made. Therefore, in the most general sense (perhaps too general for most of you to accept), the approach to economics that I am advancing extends to cover the emergence of a political constitution. At the conceptual level, this can be brought under the framework of a voluntaristic exchange process. The contract theory of the state, as well as most of the writing in that tradition, represents the sort of approach to human activity that I think modern economics should be taking.[9]

I propose to extend the system of human relationships brought within the economist's scope widely enough to include collective as well as private organization. This being so, you may ask, how are politics and economics to be distinguished? This is a proper question, and it helps me to illustrate the central point of the paper in yet another way. The distinction to be drawn between economics and poli-

---

[9] In our recent book, *The Calculus of Consent* (Ann Arbor: University of Michigan Press, 1962), Gordon Tullock and I develop the theory of the political constitution in the manner sketched out here.

tics, as disciplines, lies in the nature of the social relationships among individuals that is examined in each. Insofar as individuals exchange, trade, as freely contracting units, the predominant characteristic of their behavior is "economic." And this, of course, extends our range far beyond the ordinary price-money nexus. Insofar as individuals meet one another in a relationship of superior-inferior, leader to follower, principal to agent, the predominant characteristic in their behavior is "political,"[10] stemming, of course, from our everyday usage of the word *politician*. Economics is the study of the whole system of exchange relationships. Politics is the study of the whole system of coercive or potentially coercive relationships. In almost any particular social institution, there are elements of both types of behavior, and it is appropriate that both the economist and the political scientist study such institutions. What I should stress is the potentiality of exchange in those sociopolitical institutions that we normally regard as embodying primarily coercive or quasi-coercive elements. To the extent that man has available to him alternatives of action, he meets his associates as, in some sense, an "equal," in other words, in a trading relationship. Only in those situations where pure rent is the sole element in return is the economic relationship wholly replaced by the political.

As I have noted, almost all of the institutions and relationships that economists currently study will remain subject to examination in the disciplinary frame that I propose to draw around "economics." The same basic data are central to the allocation approach and the exchange approach.

---

[10] This distinction has been developed at some length by Gordon Tullock, *The Politics of Bureaucracy* (Washington: Public Affairs Press, 1965).

But the interpretation of these data, and even the very questions that we ask of them, will depend critically on the reference system within which we operate. What will the shift in reference system produce? The most important single result will be the making of a sharp and categorical distinction between the discipline to which our theory of markets applies and that which we may call "social engineering," for want of any better term. Note that I am not here saying that social engineering is not legitimate endeavor. I am suggesting only that the implications concerning the uses of individuals as means to nonindividual ends be explicitly recognized. My criticism of the orthodox approach to economics is based, at least in part, on its failure to allow such implications to be appropriately made. If the economic problem is viewed as the general means-ends problem, the social engineer is a working economist in the full sense of the term. Thus it is that we now observe him developing more and more complicated schemata designed to maximize more and more complex functions, under more and more specifically defined constraints. We applaud all of this as "scientific" advance, and regard the aids that we may provide for the practicing social engineer in these respects as our "social" purpose. There is, I submit, something wholly confused about all of this. I too applaud and admire the ingenuity of the applied mathematicians who have helped, and are helping, choosers to solve more complex computational problems. But I shall continue to insist that our purpose, if you will, is no more that of providing the social engineer with these tools than that of providing the monopolist with tools to make more profits, or Wicksteed's housewife with instructions how better to divide the mashed potatoes among her children. The proper role of the economist is not providing the means of making "better" choices, and to imply this, as the resource allocation-choice approach does, tends to confuse most of us at the very outset of our training.

I want to note especially here that I am not, through rejecting the allocation approach, decrying the desirability of, indeed the necessity for, mathematical competence. In fact, advances in our understanding of symbiotic relationships may well require considerably more sophisticated mathematical tools than those required in what I have called social engineering. For example, we need to learn much more about the theory of n-person cooperative games. It seems but natural that the mathematics finally required to systematize a set of relationships involving voluntary behavior of many persons will be more complicated than that required to solve even the most complex computational problem in which the ends are ordered in a single function.

Although this will, of course, be challenged, the position that I advance is neutral with respect to ideological or normative content. I am simply proposing, in various ways, that economists concentrate attention on the institutions, the relationships, among individuals as they participate in voluntarily organized activity, in trade or exchange, broadly considered. People may, as in my swamp-clearing example, decide to do things collectively. Or they may not. The analysis, as such, is neutral in respect to the proper private-sector–public-sector mix. I am stating that economists should be "market economists," but only because I think they should concentrate on market or exchange institutions, again recalling that these are to be conceived in the widest possible sense. This need not bias or prejudice them for or against any particular form of social order. Learning more about how markets work means learning more about how markets work. They may work better or worse, in terms of whatever criteria that might be imposed, than uninformed opinion leads one to expect.

To an extent, of course, we must all follow along the road that is functionally determined by the behavior of our disciplinary colleagues. The growth and development of a discipline are somewhat like language and, despite the fact that we may think that the current direction of change is misleading and productive of intellectual confusions, we must try to continue communicating with one another. It would be naive in the extreme for me to think that I could, through individual persuasion such as this, or in concert with a few others who might agree broadly with me on such matters, change the drift of a whole social science. Economics, as a well-defined subject of scholarship, seems to be disintegrating, and for the reasons I have outlined, and realistic appraisal suggests that this process will not be stopped. Nevertheless, it is useful, or so it seems to me, to stop occasionally and look at the roadmap.

I may conclude by recalling an adage that Frank Ward, of the University of Tennessee, had pinned to his office door when I first met him in 1940. I was then a very green, beginning graduate student. The adage said: "The study of economics won't keep you out of the breadline; but at least you'll know why you're there." I can paraphrase this to apply to methodology: "Concentration on methodology won't solve any of the problems for you, but at least you should know what the problems are."

2

Is Economics the Science of Choice?

From time to time it is probably necessary to detach oneself from the technicalities of the argument and to ask quite naively what it is all about.

F. A. HAYEK, *Economics and Knowledge*

Robert Mundell commences his Preface to *Man and Economics* with the assertion: "Economics is the science of choice."[1] Most professional scholars who check off the box marked "Economist" on the Register of Scientific Personnel find no quarrel with Mundell's statement. Despite some danger of once again being called iconoclastic, I propose to examine this assertion seriously and critically. In the process, I shall not discuss what economics is or is not, should or should not be, at least in any direct sense. My question is more elementary and its answer is obvious once it is asked. I want to ask whether a *science* of *choice* is possible at all. Are we not involved in a contradiction in terms?

This chapter was originally published in *Roads to Freedom: Essays in Honor of F. A. Hayek,* ed. Erich Streissler (London: Routledge & Kegan Paul, 1969), pp. 47–64. Permission to reprint is herewith acknowledged. I am indebted to David B. Johnson, Roland N. McKean, Gordon Tullock, and Richard E. Wagner for helpful comments.

[1] New York, 1968.

There is no need to go beyond the everyday usage of the two words. I am neither competent nor interested in detailed etymological inquiry. To choose means "to take by preference out of all that are available," "to select."[2] Choice is the "act of choosing," or "selecting." In particular, choosing should be distinguished from behaving. The latter implies acting but there is no reference to conscious selection from among alternatives. Behavior can be predetermined and, hence, predictable. Choice, by its nature, cannot be predetermined and remain choice. If we then define science in the modern sense of embodying conceptually refutable predictions, a science of choice becomes self-contradictory.[3]

This elementary proposition is recognized by those who accept the Mundell position. If this is the case, what are the reasons for adherence to what, at first glance, seems glaring methodological inconsistency? To the economist, choice seems to be imposed by the fact of scarcity. Given an acknowledged multiplicity of ends and a limitation on means, it becomes necessary that some selection among alternatives be made. It is in such a very general setting that economics has been classified as the study of such selection, or choice. Once that is done, replacing the word *study* with the word *science* becomes a natural extension of language. Is the science so defined devoid of predictive content? Some scholars might answer affirmatively, but surely there are many others who, at the same time that they acquiesce in Mun-

---

[2] *Oxford Universal Dictionary*, 1955.

[3] In a wholly determinist universe, choice is purely illusory, as is discussion about choice. I do not treat this age-old issue, and I prefer to think that the subject discussed as well as the discussion itself is not illusory.

dell's statement, busy themselves with the empirical testing of hypotheses. Are such professionals unaware of their methodological contradictions? It seems useful to try to answer these questions in some detail.

I The Categories of Economic Theory

1 *The Logic of Economic Choice*

The legitimacy of a "science of choice" may be questioned, but there should be no doubts about the usefulness of a "logic of choice." Much of orthodox economic theory is precisely this, and is, therefore, concerned with choice, as such. This logical theory provides students with the "economic point of view" and it can be posed in either a normative or a positive setting. In the former, the logic reduces to the economic principle, the simple requirement that returns to like units of outlay or input must be equalized at the margins in order to secure a maximum of output. In this most general sense, the principle is empirically empty. It instructs the chooser, the decision-maker, on the procedures for making selections without requiring that he define either his own preference ordering of output combinations or the resource constraints within which he must operate. Empirical emptiness should not, however, be equated with uselessness. If a potential chooser is made aware of the principle in its full import, he will weigh alternatives more carefully, he will think in marginal terms, he will make evaluations of opportunity costs, and, finally, he will search more diligently for genuine alternatives. The norms for choice can be meaningfully discussed, even if the specific implementation takes place only in the internal calculus of the decision-maker. Instructing the decision-maker as to how he should choose may produce "better" choices as evaluated by his own standards.

There is a positive counterpart to the logic of choice, and this extends theory to the interaction among separate decision-makers. Commencing with the fact that choosers choose and that they do so under constraints which include the behavior of others, the economist can begin to make meaningful statements about the results that emerge from the interaction among several choosers. Certain "laws" can be deduced, even if conceptually refutable hypotheses cannot be derived. Analysis makes no attempt to specify preference orderings for particular choosers. The "law" of choice states only that the individual decision-maker will select that alternative that stands highest on his preference ordering. Defined in purely logical terms, this produces the "law of demand." In this way, trade or exchange can be explained, even in some of its most complex varieties. Characteristics of equilibrium positions can be derived, these being defined in terms of the coordination between expected and realized plans of the separate decision-takers.

In the strictest sense, the chooser is not specified in the pure logic of choice. Under the standard assumptions, the analysis applies to the individual. But the logic requires no such limitation; it applies universally. The norms for efficient choice can be treated independently of the processes through which decisions are actually made. It is not, therefore, explicitly in error to present decision-making norms for non-existent collective entities who do not, in fact, choose. Under some conditions, it may be helpful to discuss the economizing as if such entities existed, although, as we shall note in section two, this is the source of much confusion.

In its normative variant, the logical theory of choice involves the simple principle of economizing, nothing more. This is the mathematics of maxima and minima. Much of modern economic theory is limited to various elaborations on this mathematics. By modifying the formal properties of the objective function and the constraints, interesting exercises in locating and in stating the required conditions for ensuring satisfaction of the norms can be produced. Whether or not such exercises command too much of the professional investment of modern economists remains an open question.

The logical theory of interaction among many choosers may also be classified as pure mathematics. But this mathematics is not that which has attracted major interest of the professionals in that discipline, and there is some legitimacy in the economists' preemptive claim. Game theory, as one part of a general theory of interaction, owes its origin to a mathematician, but the elegant theory of competitive equilibrium was developed by economists. Major strides are being made in this purely logical theory of interaction among many choosers, some of which are aimed at relating game theory, more generally the theory of coalition formation, to the theory of competitive equilibrium. The marginal productivity of mathematically inclined economists in this area of research appears much higher than that which is aimed at working out complex variations of the simple maximization problem.

2 *The Abstract Science of Economic Behavior*

In the logical theory summarized, no objectives are specified. Choice remains free, and because of this, it remains choice. As we move beyond this pure logic, however, and into economic theory as more generally, if ambiguously, conceived, choice becomes circumscribed. Specific motivation is imputed to the decision-maker, and it is seldom recognized that, to the extent that this takes place, genuine choice is removed from the theory. What we now confront is *behavior,* not choice, behavior that is subject to conceptually predictable laws. The entity that acts, that behaves, does so in accordance with the patterns imposed by the postulates of the theoretical science. The actor is, so to speak, programmed to behave in direct response to stimuli. The abstract science of economic behavior, as I have here classified this, has empirical content that is wholly missing in the pure logic of economic choice. This content is provided by restricting the utility function. Several degrees of restrictiveness may be imposed. Minimally, nothing more than a specification of "goods" may be introduced. From this alone, conceptually refutable hypotheses emerge. The acting-behaving unit *must* choose more of any "good" when its "price" relative to other "goods" declines.[4] Additional restrictiveness takes the form of specifying something about the internal trade-offs among goods in the utility function of the behaving unit. This step produces the *homo economicus* of classical theory who must, when confronted with alternatives, select that which stands highest on his preference ranking, as evaluated in terms of a *numéraire.* The pure economic man must behave so as to take more rather than less when confronted with simple monetary alternatives. He must maximize income-wealth and minimize outlays. He must maximize profits if he plays the role of entrepreneur.

Confusion has arisen between this abstract science of eco-

---

[4] This approach may be associated with the work of A. A. Alchian and his colleagues. See A. A. Alchian and W. R. Allen, *University Economics,* 2d ed. (Belmont, Calif., 1967).

nomic behavior and the pure logic of choice because of ambiguities that are involved in the several means of bounding the utility functions of the acting units. In the pure logic of choice, the arguments in the utility function are not identified; "goods" and "bads" are unknown to the external observer. In any science of economic behavior, the goods must be classified as such. But under minimally restricted utility functions, specific trade-offs among these may remain internal to the acting units. The individual chooses in the sense that his selection from among several desirable alternatives remains unpredictable to the observer. What we have here is an extremely limited "science" of behavior combined with an extensive "logic" of genuine choice. We move beyond this essentially mixed framework when the trade-offs are more fully specified. Additional "laws of behavior" can then be derived; and, more important, predictions can be made about the results of the interaction processes. These predictions can be conceptually refuted by empirical evidence. If internal trade-offs among goods in utility functions are fully specified, behavior becomes completely predictable in the abstract. Normal procedure does not, however, involve the extension to such limits.

As noted earlier, the pure logic of choice may be interpreted in either a normative or a positive sense. If choice is real, it is meaningful to refer to "better" and "worse" choices, and the simple maximizing principle can be of some assistance to the decision-taker. By relatively sharp contrast, there is no normative content in the abstract science of economic behavior. The reason is obvious. The acting unit responds to environmental stimuli in predictably unique fashion; there is no question as to the "should" of behavior. The unit responds and that is that. Failure to note this basic difference between the pure logic of choice and the pure science of behavior provides, I think, an explanation of the claim, advanced especially by Mises, that economic theory is a general theory of human action.[5] The logical theory is indeed general but empty; the scientific theory is nongeneral but operational.

At this point, it seems useful to refer to the distinction between the "subjectivist economics," espoused by both Mises and Hayek, and the "objectivist economics," which is more widely accepted, even if its limitations are seldom explicitly recognized. In the logic of choice, choosing becomes a subjective experience. The alternatives for choice as well as the evaluations placed upon these exist only in the mind of the decision-maker. Cost, which is the obstacle to choice, is purely subjective and this consists in the chooser's evaluation of the alternative that must be sacrificed in order to attain that which is selected. This genuine opportunity cost vanishes once a decision is taken. By relatively sharp contrast with this, in the pure science of economic behavior choice itself is illusory. In the abstract model, the behavior of the actor is predictable by an external observer. This requires that some criteria for behavior be objectively measurable, and this objectivity is supplied when the motivational postulate is plugged into the model. An actor behaves so as to maximize utility, defined in a nonempty sense. It becomes impossible, in the formal model, for an actor to "choose" less rather than more of the common denominator units, money or some *numéraire* good, when he is faced with such alternatives. Cost, in this objectivist theory, the pure science of economics, is measurable by the observer. This cost is

---

[5] See Ludwig von Mises, *Human Action* (New Haven, 1949).

unrelated to choice, as such, since the latter really does not exist. The opportunity cost of using a resource unit in one way rather than another consists in the *money* earnings of that unit in its most productive alternative use. These earnings may be objectively estimated and quantified. In this setting, the cost of a beaver is two deer, and there is no relationship between cost and sacrifice.[6] To say here that nonpecuniary elements may affect choice is to confuse the model of pure economic behavior with the model of the logic of choice. Insofar as nonpecuniary noneconomic elements actually enter the resource owner's calculus, the behavioral model is falsified.[7]

The motivational postulate, the behavior of *homo economicus*, effectively converts the purely logical theory of choice into an abstract science of behavior. It accomplishes this by replacing the subjectivity of the logical theory by objective payoffs. Generality in explanation is and must be sacrificed in crossing this bridge. But this is replaced by predictability. The abstract science of economic behavior is the familiar world of *ceteris paribus*. This science provides the analyst with tools for discussing the complex interaction of market processes to the extent that individual participants

---

[6] For an extended discussion of the concept of cost in contrasting methodological settings, see my *Cost and Choice: An Inquiry in Economic Theory* (Chicago: Markham Publishing Co., 1969).

[7] To avoid ambiguity here, I should note that nonpecuniary "goods" can be introduced in individual utility functions in the minimally restricted limits that were discussed above. Given the specification of such goods, conceptually refutable hypotheses about individual behavior can be derived. Nonpecuniary goods tend to be different for different individuals, however, and the limits of any predictive science are reached when those goods which are common to all persons are exhausted. This provides the basis for reliance on the strictly pecuniary motivation in the general model of the economic interaction process.

behave economically. Equilibrium characteristics can be objectively described in terms of quantifiable, measurable relationships among variables, among prices and costs. It is this abstract theory upon which most economists rely in making rudimentary predictions about reality. When asked, "What will happen when an excise tax is placed on product X?" the professional responds: "The price of X to consumers will rise, and less will be demanded, provided that other things remain unchanged, and provided that men behave economically." The last qualifying phrase, "provided that men behave economically," shifts the analysis into the science of behavior and enables conceptually refutable predictions to be advanced. By this qualifier, the economist states that he is preventing actors from behaving other than economically in the theoretical model that he is constructing. As we all recognize, many professionals do not go further than this; they do not consider it a part of their task either to examine the psychology of behavior more fully or to test empirically the predictions that the abstract science enables them to make.

Such methodological aloofness is acceptable only so long as the severe limitations of the scientist's role are appreciated. Failure to recognize these limitations leads naive professionals to claim far too much for the science and with such claims they infuriate those critics who concentrate attention on the noneconomic content in human choice patterns.

3 The Predictive Science of Economic Behavior

The abstract science is restricted to the derivation of propositions or hypotheses that are conceptually refutable. The realm of predictive science is entered only when these hypotheses are subjected to empirical testing against real-world observations. One of the features of modern economic research has been its shift toward the rigorous testing of hypotheses. The pound of *ceteris paribus* no longer protects the scientist; he must, through imaginative construction of hypotheses and through exhaustive search for appropriate data, try to corroborate the predictions that the theory allows him to make. Because of empirical constraints, the range of his efforts must be more limited than that allowed to the free-floating abstract theorist. Data are difficult to come by, and even when these can be assembled, the hypotheses tester must be prepared for frustration and failure. Data can, at best, reflect the results of genuine choices made by participants in a very complicated interaction sequence. The economic behavior implicit in these choices may be nonexistent in some cases, and swamped in effect by noneconomic considerations in many others. The predictive hypotheses may be refuted at the initial levels of testing. But the scientist cannot readily use such refutation for overthrowing the general laws of behavior derived from the central structure of his theory. He must normally acknowledge his probable failure to isolate the economic from the noneconomic elements of choice, and, accordingly, he must acknowledge the continuing challenge of empirical testability for his theoretically based hypotheses.

This amounts to saying that, despite his efforts, the predictive scientist remains chained to the vision of the economic universe produced in the abstract theory of economic behavior. He can, when successful, show that indeed "water runs down hill," but, with contrary results, he can rarely, if ever, refute the economic analogue to the law of gravity. At best, the predictive science is an extension of the abstract science. It must incorporate the basic motivational postulate of *homo economicus;* indeed this provides the source for deriving the hypotheses to be tested. The paradigms are unchanged over the two subdisciplines.

There are, however, significant differences. In some strict sense, the abstract science treats only of pure economic man, unalloyed by noneconomic behavioral traits. Accordingly, the theorems are simple, elegant and aesthetically satisfying. But the real world is a grubby place, and it is this world that must be the raw source for any science that aims at operational validity. In the face of the apparent divergence of the real world from the paradigms of the abstract science, the empirical corroboration of many predictive hypotheses is perhaps surprising.

The fact that his hypotheses refer to the behavior of *many* actors greatly facilitates the predictive scientist's efforts. He need only make predictions about the behavior of average or representative participants in the processes that he observes; he need not hypothesize about the behavior of any single actor. Hence even if noneconomic elements dominate the behavior of some participants, and even if these enter to some degree in the choices of all participants, given certain symmetry in the distributions of preferences, the hypotheses derived from the abstract theory may still be corroborated. For example, given comparable institutional constraints, the wage levels for plumbers and carpenters may tend toward equality even if a substantial proportion of plumbers exhibit strong noneconomic preferences for their chosen occupation and even if a substantial proportion of carpenters exhibit similar preferences for their own occupation. So long as some sufficient number of persons indicates some willingness to make the occupational shift on purely economic grounds, the hypothesis about wage level equality is supported. The multiplicity of participants generates results that are identical to those predicted in the model that embodies the strict assumption that all actors behave economically.

4 The "Behavioristic" Science of the Economy

Unless he is able to call upon the motivational postulate of the abstract science, the predictive scientist can scarcely derive the hypotheses that he seeks to test. It is folly for him to abandon this postulate deliberately in some misguided attempt at imitating the methods of the natural scientists who find it impossible to introduce comparable behavioral postulates. "Scientism" of this sort has been effectively criticized by Hayek[8] and others, and this approach need not be examined in detail here. It seems clear that with no behavioral basis from which to begin his search for uniformities and regularities in the data that he observes, the pure "behaviorist" is reduced to massive efforts at observation with very limited prospects of successful results. He confronts a universe of prices, quantities, employment levels, measures for national aggregates. He presumably remains aloof from the behavior that generates these data as results, whether this behavior be economic or not. This is not to suggest that such efforts should be wholly abandoned. It seems clear, however, that the deliberate sacrifice of the directional hypotheses provided by the paradigms of economic science should be made with great caution.

A somewhat different behaviorist approach (and one that fits the terminology considerably better) involves an

---

[8] F. A. Hayek, *The Counter-Revolution of Science* (Indianapolis: Liberty Fund, 1979).

attempt to specify noneconomic elements that enter into the individual's choice calculus. This approach, which we may associate with the work of Herbert A. Simon and his colleagues,[9] calls upon psychological insight to assist in the development of motivational patterns that may be considerably more complex than the simple postulates of standard economic theory. Ultimately, the objective parallels those of orthodox economic science, the ability to make predictions about human behavior in the social interaction process. And, to the extent that the hypotheses of standard theory are refuted, such an approach as this offers the only avenue of advance for social science. This approach may proceed by relaxing or modifying the restrictions placed on individual utility functions, or, alternatively, the procedure may involve dropping the utilitarian framework.[10]

II The Confusions of Economic Theory

Economics, as this discipline is currently interpreted, embodies elements of each of the four categories listed. The confusions arise from the failure of economists to understand the categorical distinctions. Many of the continuing and unresolved arguments over particular methodological issues can be traced more or less directly to this source.

1 *The Derivation of Policy Norms*

One of these arguments concerns the relevance of theory for deriving policy conclusions. I shall illustrate some of

---

[9] H. A. Simon, *Models of Man* (New York, 1957).

[10] This summary review does not do justice to the approach under discussion. For the most part, the contributions here have been made by social scientists in disciplines other than economics. Indeed, to the extent that social "science" other than economics exists at all, it must be produced by those who adopt the approach summarized here.

the confusion here through the familiar prisoner's dilemma of game theory, interpreted variously in terms of the categories of Section I. The pedagogic advantages of this construction are immense; properly employed the dilemma allows us to introduce in a two-person interaction model many of the relevent issues of economic policy in the large.

The illustration below presents the dilemma in a form slightly modified from its classic setting. The game depicted is positive-sum. The first term in each cell indicates the payoff to A, the player who chooses between rows. The second term shows the payoff to B, the player who chooses between columns. Each player's result depends on the behavior of the other, but, for each player, there is a dominating strategy shown by the second row and second column. The independent-behavior solution, shown in the southeast cell of the matrix, depicts the dilemma; the combined payoffs are larger in the northwest cell.

Player B

Player A	50, 50	20, 60
	60, 20	30, 30

With nothing more than the payoff matrix of the illustration, something has been said about the interaction of the two players. Their choice behavior has been related to the structure of the game itself, and the possible conflict between the independent-adjustment solution and the combined-payoff potential outcome has been shown. Nonetheless, it should be noted that, to this point, nothing has been said about the nature of the payoffs. These have been treated strictly as numerical indicators of that which motivates choice behavior. In some respects, these payoffs may be thought of as being defined in utility units, so long as the purely subjective nature of utility in this context is kept in mind. In this setting, we have remained strictly in the pure logic of choice. There is absolutely no predictive content in the analysis.[11]

We move from this pure logic of choice into the abstract science of economic behavior when we define the payoffs objectively. To do this, we need only to put dollar signs in front of the numbers in the matrix illustration. The solution seems to remain as before, but it is now limited to those situations where players do, in fact, behave economically. There will be no convergence to the southeast cell if players in the real world should choose to behave cooperatively rather than independently. The abstract theory of economics says that they will behave economically, that the southeast cell is the "solution" to the game. This prediction may be falsified, at least conceptually.

At this level, it becomes legitimate to derive limited policy implications from the analysis. As they behave in the real world, individuals are observed to adopt the dominating strategies, as these are identified in the eyes of the observer. In the objectified payoff structure imputed to the participants, there appears to exist a conflict between the independent-adjustment outcome and the jointly desired

---

[11] See John C. Harsanyi, "A General Theory of Rational Behavior in Game Situations," *Econometrica* 34 (1966): 613 f.

optimal outcome. Given nothing more than the potentiality of this conflict, it becomes plausible for the political economist to consider modifications in the choice structure that would enable individual participants to eliminate such a conflict, if indeed it should exist. If ways and means can be found to remove the restrictions of the potential dilemma, if institutional rearrangements can be made which will allow independent behavior of the participants to produce results that may be mutually more beneficial than those observed under present environmental conditions, these should, of course, be suggested. (In the strict prisoner's dilemma example, and limiting attention to the world of the two prisoners only, the introduction of communication between the two persons represents such an institutional change.) This point was recognized and well expressed by Sir Dennis Robertson when he called upon the economist to suggest ways to minimize the use of "that scarce resource Love."[12] Since Adam Smith, economists have been within the bounds of methodological propriety when they have proposed organizational-institutional arrangements that channel behavior that may be, but need not be, economically motivated in the direction of promoting what may be, but need not be, mutually desired economic objectives.

This very general policy position, which I shall call Smithean, requires minimal empirical backing along with minimal ethical content. All that is required is the conceptual possibility that payoffs relevant for individual behavior should be directionally linked with those emerging from the postulate of economic science. So long as a person may, other things

---

[12] D. H. Robertson, "What Does the Economist Economize?" in *Economic Commentaries* (London, 1956).

equal, respond to the change in stimuli, as objectified, in the direction suggested by the central postulate of the theory, the economist is justified in his search for institutional arrangements that will remove the restrictiveness of the dilemma, should it exist. In a very general sense, this amounts to little more than opening up avenues for potential trades which participants may or may not find it advantageous to exploit. The policy prescription is, in effect, limited to suggestions for widening the range for potential choice.[13]

To the extent that the empirical testing of hypotheses supports the central behavioral postulate of the abstract theory, the productivity of Smithean institutional reforms is enhanced. But the corroboration of the behavioral postulate by empirical evidence implies much more than the *ceteris paribus* limits of the abstract theory. Such corroboration indicates that economic behavior dominates all noneconomic elements of choice in the specific context examined. This offers a temptation to go much beyond the general institutional reforms implied by the Smithean position. If man can be shown to behave in some more direct relationship to an objectified payoff structure than the *ceteris paribus* potentiality implied by the abstract theory, direct manipulation of his behavior seems to become possible through the appropriate modification in the conditions for choice. It is one thing to say that, when given the opportunity, an individual will choose more rather than less provided other elements affecting his choice remain unchanged. It becomes quite a different thing to say that the representative indi-

---

[13] For an earlier and somewhat different statement of this position, see my "Positive Economics, Welfare Economics, and Political Economy," *Journal of Law and Economics* 2 (October 1959): 124–38; reprinted in *Fiscal Theory and Political Economy* (Chapel Hill, 1960).

vidual will choose more rather than less in terms of objectified units in the *numéraire* without regard to noneconomic influences on his choice situation. Rarely will the multidimensional complexity of real-world choice allow results of such simplicity to be adduced. But, if it should do so, specific control of individual behavior through imposed changes in the payoff structures might be possible.

It is precisely at this point that a pervasive and fundamental error emerges. The false step is taken when the explicitly objectified payoff structure that is postulated for use in the abstract theory of economic behavior is translated into direct guidelines for the explicit manipulation of choice alternatives. This procedure must assume that the actual *choice-maker* in the real world *behaves* strictly as the pure economic man of the theorist's model. Markets are held to "fail" because of the dilemma-type situations that are confronted by the idealized man of the theorist's analytical model. As a followup to this, policy suggestions are made which incorporate this rarefied behavioral postulate as reality. In a genuine sense, this whole procedure is absurd.

The point can be illustrated with the matrix of the illustration. The abstract theory bases its elaboration of the interaction processes on the postulate that individuals behave economically in the sense that they respond to objectified and externally measurable payoffs. In this context, it is meaningful to say that, in the model, player A selects row 2 rather than row 1 because of the $10 difference in payoff, regardless of what he predicts about B's behavior. It is meaningful to say that, in this model, the opportunity cost to player A, "that which could be avoided by his not taking row 2," is $10 in foregone payoffs. But this opportunity cost, embodied in the theoretical model for behavior, cannot then be taken as the specific basis for policy prescription aimed at manipulating A's actual choice behavior. This violates the purpose and meaning of the abstract theory and, as suggested, has little or no empirical base. Despite this, such procedure is manifest in a substantial part of modern economic policy discussion.

It is not caricature to say that modern policy discussion, which I shall call Pigovian, proceeds as follows, still within the matrix illustration. The economist proposes a "corrective" tax on player A, a tax designed to make the costs that he privately confronts equivalent to those that are confronted by the collectivity in the two alternatives that are faced. The general welfare criterion becomes equality between *private* and *social* cost. To implement this result, private costs must be modified; but in order to know by how much, some assumption must be made about private payoff structures. The orthodoxy proceeds as if the purely economic man existed. The criterion calls for a tax of $10+ to be imposed on A's returns in row 2 (or a subsidy of $10+ on his returns in row 1). Given this change in his alternatives, player A (similarly for player B) will be motivated to "choose" that alternative that is jointly desired. The efficient collective outcome will be generated. The emphasis has been subtly shifted from the exploitation of potential gains-from-trade to the attaining of specifically defined results.

As the construction shows, if either A or B should behave noneconomically the suggested modification of the payoff matrix may not produce the desired results. Suppose, for example, that both players value independent action highly and are willing to sacrifice economic gain to secure this objective. In this instance, the independent-adjustment solution in the southeast cell remains dominant, regardless of the imposition of the suggested corrective tax or subsidy. Some tax (or subsidy) will, of course, result in behavioral change, but the outcome may be less rather than more desirable in some "social" sense. The dilemma indicated to be present in objectified payoff structure may not exist when payoffs relevant to genuine choices are incorporated in the matrix. The artificiality of any objectified payoff structure, as conceived by the external observer, tends to be overlooked with the consequence that "dilemmas" which exist only in the mind of the observer may be imputed to actual participants in an interaction process.

The point of emphasis is clear. The costs that influence "choice" are purely subjective and these exist only within the mind of the decision-maker. The economist may, within limits, discuss this choice provided that he remains within what we have called the "logic of choice." He cannot, however, plug in the *homo economicus* introduced in his abstract models of economic behavior and then use this as the basis for constructing specific choice-influencing constraints aimed at welfare improvements. Individuals choose on the basis of their own preference orderings; they may, within limits, behave as the abstract theory of economics postulates. But rarely do they behave strictly as the automatons of the analytical models. Yet this is precisely the unrecognized assumption that is implicit in most modern policy discussion.

The critical distinction to be made is that between what I have called the Smithean policy position and what I have called the Pigovian policy norms. In the former, organizational-institutional changes, modifications in the structure of property rights, require only that possible conflicts between individually adjusted behavior and mutually desired collective outcomes be recognized. Specific definition of "efficient" or "optimal" results is not needed. Such results are allowed to emerge from the choice process itself. In the Pigovian framework, by contrast, property rights are normally assumed to be fixed exogenously. Corrective measures take the form of specific modifications in the choice conditions that are confronted by individual participants. Clearly, this approach to policy requires much more knowledge about the actual preference orderings of individuals. Efficiency in outcomes is no longer defined by the observed absence of further gains from trade as revealed by the behavior of traders. This Smithean definition is replaced by the objectively defined set of equalities central to theoretical welfare economics.

The error extends through much of modern economics. This was at the base of the debate over the possibility of socialist calculation that took place in the 1930s. Mises and Hayek were, I think, indirectly making essentially the same point that I have tried to make here. Their arguments failed to convince their fellow economists; most economists continue to think that efficiency, at least ideally, can be produced by the enforcement of output and pricing *rules,* that these can effectively substitute for the modification in *property rights* dictated by the particular economic setting.

2 *"Scientific" Decision-Making for the Collectivity: Systems Analysis, Operations Research, Cost-Benefit Analysis*

The confusions embodied in the Pigovian norms are complemented by an even more elementary set of confusions when the economist extends his range to the "choices" of the collectivity. He tends to be trapped in the scarcity-choice maximization nexus, and it is not at all easy for him to accept the fact that a collective "decision-maker" or "chooser" is nonexistent. Failing this, he tends to conceptualize some supraindividual entity which makes effective choices, which maximizes some objective function subject to appropriately defined constraints. This procedure allows the analyst to produce interesting and self-satisfying results. But error arises when either the analyst or his interpreters consider such results applicable to real-world issues.

Analysis of this sort is two dimensions away from real-world relevance. In the first place, the "logic of choice" for the single decision-maker is applied to a situation where no such person or entity exists. Since there is no maximizer, analysis is of questionable value when it is based on the assumption that one exists.[14] In the second place, the costs and benefits of alternative courses of action must be objectified if the analyst is to do more than present his own value orderings. This objectification runs into the same difficulty as that noted in connection with the Pigovian approach. There may be little or no relationship between the objectively defined costs and benefits and the evaluations that individuals place on alternatives in actual choice situations.

In this latter respect, the analyst has even less to fall back on than the Pigovian welfare economist. The abstract science of economic behavior with its embodiment of economic man does provide some basis for considering modifications in the conditions of choice, as faced by acting persons. For the cost-benefit analyst, however, there is no prospect of

---

[14] These comments apply only to the orthodox analyses under discussion here. It is possible to advance understanding of actual processes of group decision-making through an extension of the pure logic of choice applied to individual participants in these processes. In this approach, there need be no presumption that the collectivity, as such, maximizes anything, or indeed itself exists.

modifying the alternatives facing individual choosers. He must advance norms for choice itself. He is advising the collectivity quite specifically concerning how it "should" choose. Even if the complexities of group decision-making are ignored, the subjective evaluations of individuals are of a different dimension from the objectively quantifiable measurements placed on alternatives by the analyst. And it should be emphasized here that this difficulty is not removed by allowing the careful analyst to introduce "nonquantifiable" elements into his calculus. In point of fact, the more subjective that his own calculus becomes, the *less* relevent become his efforts. At best, he may be able to place values on cost and benefit streams that would characterize the world in which all men behave economically. This calculus would be of limited, but perhaps of positive value. Once this standard drawn from the behavioral postulate of the abstract science is left behind, however, there is nothing that the analyst can provide that assists in the understanding of actual collective decision processes.

III Conclusions

Modern economics, as practiced by professional scholars, embodies confusions that are fundamentally methodological. These have their historical foundations in the failure of economists to establish an effective synthesis between the objective and the subjective theory of value. The issues did not emerge with clarity, however, until efforts were made to extend the applicability of economic theory beyond its traditional limits. So long as the task of theory remained that of "explaining" the functioning of a market system, objective and subjective elements could exist side by side without open contradiction. During the past half-century, however, theory has been called upon to do much more than this. It has been employed to derive norms for policy aimed at making allocation more "efficient." Economists have, in other words, proceeded as if theirs were a "science of choice."

It is in such extensions that the confusions that I have stressed in this paper have emerged. The critical methodological oversight was that which Hayek emphasized, with clarity but to little avail, in several of his fundamental papers in the late 1930s and early 1940s. The failure of economists to recognize that the sense data upon which individuals actually choose in either market or political choice structures are dimensionally distinct from any data that can be objectively called upon by external observers led directly to the methodological chaos that currently exists. Economics seems unlikely to escape from this chaos for many years, if indeed it survives at all as an independent discipline. Few economists are wholly free of the confusions that I have discussed. For myself, I advance no claim that my own thinking has yet fully rid itself of the paradigms of neoclassical orthodoxy.

3

Professor Alchian on Economic Method

In chapter two I argued that economists have failed to distinguish their methodological categories. Specifically, I distinguished among (1) a logic of economic choice, (2) an abstract science of economic behavior, and (3) a predictive science of economic behavior. In the first of these categories, no attempt is made to incorporate empirical reality; no identification of "goods" is made; no predictive hypotheses emerge. What we get is a *general* theory of human action, or choice, as von Mises argues, but because it is general it must remain nonoperational and empirically empty. In the second category, which I call the "abstract science of economic behavior" and which I, personally, associate with the thinking of Frank Knight, we move beyond strict logical limits. Here we do plug in some aspects of reality and by so doing we ensure that actors behave, not *choose*, and that they do so in a directed fashion. Here *homo economicus* comes into his own, and economic moti-

This chapter was initially developed for a seminar presentation at the University of California, Los Angeles, in November 1969. For obvious reasons, I used some of Professor Alchian's work as a target for a more generalized criticism of economic method.

vation serves as the driving behavioral force. At an abstract level, hypotheses derived are conceptually refutable. If men behave economically, predictions can be falsified. But we know that economic motivation is not pervasive over all human behavior. We know that men do choose. Hence, Knight was willing to draw limits on the explanatory potential of economic theory, limits that are short of empirical falsification. My third category, the "predictive science of economic behavior," involves a shift beyond Knight's limits, a shift to the development of hypotheses that are empirically testable.

I am not going to repeat here the argument of chapter two. I do propose to call into question one aspect of my categorization. In that discussion, I placed what might be called the "Alchian approach" squarely within the science of behavior, one or the other of the last two categories mentioned above. I am now wondering whether or not it belongs there or in the first category, the pure logic of choice. To put matters dramatically, let me pose the question: Is the Alchian approach empirically empty? Is there any positive content in it?

Let me first specify what I understand by the Alchian approach, which may not, of course, square with what Professor Alchian himself believes it to be. Alchian appears to go beyond any mere logic of choice by his apparent identification of "goods." He seems to commence analysis with an identification of goods in the individual's utility function. He specifically warns, however, that these goods are not to be constrained to that set which might be construed as narrowly "economic." The utility function of the actor is extended to include such things as "prestige, power, friends, love, respect, self-expression, talent, liberty, knowledge, good looks, leisure . . . the welfare of other people."[1] But what are the effective limits to such an extension? I may be misinterpreting him here, but Professor Alchian seems to leave his utility functions open-ended, so to speak, to allow almost any argument to be included so long as it qualifies as a good. But how does he define a good? The answer here is not clear, but he seems to do so by observing human behavior and by labeling a good anything upon which men are generally observed to place value; that is, as anything for which men demonstrate a willingness to pay a price, anything for which men seem willing to bear a cost in terms of sacrificed alternatives. Having so defined goods, Alchian then proceeds to develop the law of demand, or Postulate No. 5 in *University Economics,* which Alchian and Allen declare to be "an extremely powerful proposition." I wonder! It now seems to me that Alchian comes perilously close to defining a good as that for which the first law of demand applies and then holds up the latter as an extremely powerful proposition.

Let me acknowledge my own confusion here, but let me try to indicate some of my worries. Suppose that I am observed to place dimes in the apple machine and get apples in return. Does this observation alone indicate that apples are a good in my utility function? Is it not possible that my observed actions merely represent the disposal of "bads," in

---

[1] A. A. Alchian and W. R. Allen, *University Economics,* 2d ed. (Belmont, Calif.: Wadsworth Press, 1968), p. 16. Perhaps my critique and discussion should be directed at the Alchian-Allen approach. I limit discussion to Alchian here because I attribute to him the relevant methodology subjected to criticism here.

this case, dimes, not the securing of goods. Both apples and dimes may be bads to me, and the only means of disposing of one bad may be to take on another one. The observed behavior at this level of treatment would be identical in the two cases. We must have something other than this observation to make our identification of goods. The additional requirement may be the observation that more apples are taken when the prices are reduced. When you observe that I take more apples per week when the price per apple falls from a dime to a nickel, this does, in fact, tell you that both apples and dimes are goods in my utility function. If they were bads, I should be observed to do just the opposite.

It seems to me clear that in order to make the law of demand into the powerful proposition that Alchian wants it to be, he must introduce, at some point in his construction, *external* criteria of identification or definition for goods. He cannot rely on subjectively generated criteria to make the identification of goods which are then employed to derive predictive hypotheses about behavior. The external source in *homo economicus* is apparently straightforward (at least on the producing or supply side; things are much more fuzzy on the consuming or demand side). Alchian, however, along with many other economists, does not really want to work within the constraints imposed by the *homo economicus* assumptions about human motivation. He seeks to explain behavior that remains outside the explanatory potential of the limited set of hypotheses derivable from the behavior of simple economic man. He apparently accomplishes his objective by allowing the set of goods to be expanded to include many things vulgarly classified as "noneconomic." No objection can be raised to this procedure at all so long as precise identification is made and so long as it is clear that this identification is made on the basis of criteria other than the behavior that is to be predicted or explained in the first place.

This step need not necessarily be difficult in particular applications. Most men do value pretty secretaries, and "prettiness" can be objectively measured. Hence, the famous Alchian prediction that nonprofit institutions will be observed to employ relatively more pretty secretaries can be falsified. But just what hypothesis is being tested? That men place value on pretty secretaries? What is there about the law of demand that adds anything to this? If men value something, the so-called law of demand seems redundant; it is excess baggage, so to speak. Is this what Frank Knight really meant when he talked about economists' proving that water runs downhill?

Let us suppose, however, that these minor quibbles are neglected, and that we are able, successfully, to identify externally the set of goods in individuals' utility functions. So long as our observations indicate that men seek the good and shun the bad, so identified, can we then say they are behaving economically? What content is there left in the term *economic behavior* here?

Let me tell you how I got into all this. Consider the following example. Suppose that a person has finished his picnic lunch on a public beach and that he has some refuse or garbage to dump somewhere. He knows that a refuse bin is a half-mile down the beach. He also knows that no overt sanctions will be imposed on him if he litters the beach by simply dumping the refuse nearby. Can economic theory help us in providing an explanatory hypothesis about his behavior? Both an unlittered beach and time may be goods in the individual's utility function. But we cannot say anything at all about which alternative he values more highly, anything at all about his subjective rate of trade-off between the two goods. We can, however, introduce apparent operational content by allowing the trade-off that he confronts to be modified and by observing his change in behavior. Suppose, now, that the refuse bin is removed to one mile down the beach. We can then hypothesize that relatively more litter will be dumped on the sand and less in the refuse bin. This behavior may, it seems, be plausibly classified as "economic."

To this point there should be no quarrel. However, we should note that we have implicitly accepted a somewhat strange usage of the word *economic* to describe behavior here. We are not necessarily observing the old Adam that is *homo economicus.* Interestingly, to me at least, a person who, in his every act, behaves in strict accordance with the Kantian generalization principle would also behave "economically" in this context. So long as *both* the unlittered beach and time are goods in his utility function, he will obey the law of demand in his behavior. The pure Kantian will, at some point, dump refuse on the sand rather than walk to the refuse bin, even when he generalizes his behavior to all members of the community. This suggests that we are unable, as economic theorists, to develop hypotheses that will allow us to distinguish by behavioral observation between those persons who act according to their own narrow self-interest and those that behave in accordance with the ethical principles laid down by Kant.

This has extremely important implications for the discussion of policy. If men do, in fact, behave in accordance with some version of the Kantian imperative, potential externalities, in the normal usage of this term, will tend to be internalized within the calculus of the actors. Individuals will tend to take into account the effects of their own actions on the situation of others than themselves. Hence, in such a world there can be no need for corrective collective or governmental intervention in the private decision processes. It becomes impossible to observe "market failure" in the standard sense. We simply have no means of determining the extent to which men as they are actually behaving are internalizing potential externalities.

I doubt that any objections can be raised at this point, but it does seem plausible to hope for a somewhat more restrictive economic theory, one that might allow a distinction between "economic" and "noneconomic" behavior, between narrow self-interest and enlightened self-interest. To do this we must move outside and beyond the Alchian limits. We must do something more than identify "goods" in the utility function. We must say something specifically about the subjective trade-offs among such "goods." We should, somehow, like to be able to say that the person behaves *economically* when he is observed to dump the litter on the sand and to say that he behaves *noneconomically* when he walks all the way to the refuse bin. But this step is a difficult one to take. Just how much need the payoffs vary to enable us to say where "economic" behavior stops and "socially responsible" behavior begins? And vice versa? Once we plug in some numbers, even if we could do so, we are already perhaps beyond the limits of absurdity.

Some of this can be illustrated by numbers in the familiar prisoners' dilemma setting, discussed in chapter two. Consider the matrix:

	B	
A	1	2
1	50,50	20,60
2	60,20	30,30

As shown, the matrix has no empirical content at all since the numbers that represent positive payoffs to A and to B from actions 1 and 2 can be in "utils." We must plug in some external meaning to the payoffs. Suppose we put dollar signs in front of the numbers. This allows us to make positive and quite specific predictions about behavior. Both A and B will follow strategy 2; if they do not, the hypothesis predicting strict economic behavior is falsified. So long as the payoff to an individual from one course of action exceeds that expected from another course of action, we predict that he will adopt that course of action. He will select the *highest* payoff. This is simple, direct, operational. This is *homo economicus.* Despite the fact that, in the matrix illustration, both 1 and 2 yield expected goods in both A's and B's utility functions, the conversion of these into numerical value indicators allows us to make specific predictions that can be tested against observations. If Kantian rules of behavior should prevail, the hypothesis is falsified. The economist's predictive science breaks down.

Something of this nature seems to have been in the minds of those who have criticized economic theory and economic science. As economists, I think that we may have been too defensive and defensive in the wrong way. We have been too prone to respond to the Carlyle-Ruskin criticism by saying that our behavioral assumptions are much less restrictive than the naive criticism implies. We retreat from the attack by saying that, after all, we can explain behavior regarding such goods as the well-being of others, cultural and social relationships, etc. As we have moved defensively in this direction, I think that we have often lost sight of the drainage of predictive content from our science. Would it not have been better to adopt the Frank Knight defense? That is, to admit, openly and directly, that economic behavior is only one aspect of man's reality; to accept the limits of our science, and to accept the role of scientific isolationists rather than that of scientific imperialists.

In the more restricted domain of *homo economicus,* we can define market failure. Indeed, markets *necessarily* fail when the joint or social maximum exceeds the sum of private maxima, as externally objectified and measured. The prisoners necessarily confess. The political economist's role is clear; he identifies instances of market failure. He sorts out the various sorts of externalities. And, much more than this, he can lay down directions of adjustment that are required to produce efficiency. He can make quite specific proposals for correction. The firm with the smoking chimney can be assessed for the damages caused to the laundries of the neighborhood housewives. And this is all there is to it. The answers fall out readily from the model, and systematic correction for pervasive market failure requires only the turning of a few relevant cranks in the machine of economic theory.

The obvious difficulty in all this is that the modern welfare economist has been all too ready to do just what I have suggested, almost in caricature, without having bothered at all to inform himself about the implicit motivational assumptions of his model. He must adopt *homo economicus* in a very strictly defined sense. And, if men behave this way in market interactions, what basis is there for presuming that they behave differently in nonmarket interactions, and specifically those that will be required for carrying out the corrections for market failure. Empirical evidence drawn from the observations of "economic" behavior in the general and noneconomic Alchian methodological world provides no basis for judgment about the usefulness of the market failure models which are based on normally restrictive economic motivational assumptions.

It seems to me that rather early in the game a conflict emerges between the use and the abuse of economic theory in a *predictive scientific* sense, and its use in what we may call an *explanatory* sense. If I may speak loosely here, we may think of a tradition stemming from the classical economists and running through Marshall to Friedman and the other modern positivists, a tradition that is essentially predictive. On the other hand, and by comparison and contrast, we can think of a tradition with some classical roots also but extending directly from the Austrians, and notably through Wicksteed, Knight, Hayek, and Mises, in which tradition the role of economic theory is largely if not wholly *explanatory*. The main point of this paper is to raise the question: Where does Professor Alchian fit in all this? His position, if I interpret him correctly, seems to face both ways. He appears to seek directly testable implications of his theory, and in this sense he seems to stress predictive content. Yet, as I have indicated, he extends the motivational hypotheses so broadly as to make effective refutation of hypotheses extremely difficult if not impossible.

The whole discussion could, however, be treated as an essay in my own confusion. I find myself simultaneously being pulled in both directions, and I suspect that critics may classify some of my works as falling within one camp and some as falling within the other. On the one hand, I can appreciate the merit in restricting utility functions so that market failure becomes a meaningful prediction in some objectively measurable sense. The whole theory of externality does tell us something about markets, something that should allow us to make predictions. At the same time, however, this same theory should also be extended to tell us something about government failure. And the theory of political externality should enable us to make predictions about the behavior of individuals in nonmarket settings. We should not be allowed to have it both ways, as seems to have been characteristic of many modern welfare economists. We should not be allowed to restrict the utility function of individual actors in the market setting, including those interactions that embody externalities, and then treat the utility function of these same actors as completely open-ended when they are placed in political decision-making roles. The diagnosticians of market failure seem to me to be duty-bound to diagnose political or governmental failure.

On the other hand, I can appreciate the explanatory power that is forthcoming when we allow utility functions to incorporate as goods almost anything that might motivate persons to act. There is a genuine aesthetic satisfaction in being able to say that the tools of economic theory remain applicable over noneconomic ranges of human behavior, to be able to respond to those critics who charge us with purveying crass materialism that exploits and isolates the worst motives in the human breast. And the explanatory potential is, I think, real. Men require a vision of the social order in which they live, and the "economic point of view" can be instrumental in providing persons with a vision of social order that is not chaotic, uncontrolled, and unplanned. This suggests, of course, that economic science or economic theory serves a didactic purpose, as we all must recognize. And in one sense, modern welfare economics represents a shift from the didactic theory of classical and neoclassical economics. It is therefore understandable that this modern attack on the classical paradigms finds its roots in Marshallian economic science, translated most directly through Pigou and all of the post-Pigovians, which science includes most of us in one form or another.

We can expand the explanatory potential of economic theory, however, only at a cost. Let me take the economics of charity or income redistribution as an example. There is now considerable research work, both theoretical and empirical, devoted to the economic theory of income transfers, private and public. Almost all of the scholars working in this field commence with an attack on the neoclassical dichotomy between resource allocation and income distribution. They point out that charitable motives are present in human beings, and that utility functions can readily be expanded to include arguments for the income levels of others (in money or kind, or in utility levels themselves). From this, they proceed to set up plausible models that allow equilibrium conditions to be defined, that allow institutional structures to be examined, and predictions about institutional changes to be made. As suggested, this sort of discussion is helpfully explanatory. It is satisfying to be able to *understand* charity, with the tools of simple economic theory.

The cost of this extension is not so evident, but it must be recognized nonetheless. We can "explain" charity by an extension of the economist's model, and we can remain in predictive limits when we "explain" the market's failure to provide the "public good." But we cannot, as a next step, also explain the governmental redistribution that we observe to take place as reflecting the revealed preferences of persons for income redistribution and then, in turn, use this for either normative or predictive purposes. If the economist extends his own professional tools to explain this behavior, to produce an understanding of this behavior, the same economist cannot then use these tools as instruments of control, even in the most indirect sense. (The error here is pervasive in many areas of economics. It is often made by students of socialist planning, as pointed out by Craig Roberts, when they try to derive the objective function from the revealed behavior of the planners and then, in turn, use the objective function so derived for making statements that are thought to take the form of normatively meaningful advice.)

For the economist who utilizes *homo economicus,* who can identify market failure, I have suggested above that he is under an obligation to identify government or political failure. For the economist who drops *homo economicus* in favor of an open-ended utility function, no failure can be recognized. He cannot identify market failure, but neither can he identify government or political failure. It is as much of a sin for von Mises or his followers to decry government failure on the basis of their empirically empty model as it is for Bator to neglect governmental failure in his extremely restricted model.

I feel much of the same ambivalence toward the explicit introduction of transactions costs into the body of economic theory. There is much explanatory potential in the transactions-cost notion, and it helps us to *understand* aspects of observed economic reality. Just as with the extended utility functions, however, the additional understanding comes at a cost. Scientific predictive content in the theory is reduced; the whole structure of analysis becomes less discriminating in the predictions it can make. If men behave economically, and if transactions costs can be neglected, our tools enable us to predict that prices paid by all buyers in a market for a physically homogeneous commodity will be equivalent. If we allow our actors to behave differently, to consider nonpecuniary aspects of the buying relationship, for example, the prettiness of the salesgirls, or if we allow transactions costs to make retrading inefficient, this central theorem of price equivalence cannot be tested. When we observe the absence of price uniformity, should we retreat into the generalized escape routes or should we simply admit the limitations of our science? As I have indicated, I do not think that the arguments are all on one side here.

I am reminded of George Stigler's early paper on built-in flexibility and average cost curves. He explained, you will recall, how profit-maximizing firms which face demand and output uncertainties may find it advantageous to build plants so that they will remain tolerably efficient at many levels of output rather than optimally efficient over much narrower ranges. The analogy with economic science seems close. We do increase, and substantially so, the explanatory flexibility of economic science when we incorporate such things as open-ended utility functions, transactions costs, threshold-sensitive behavior. But in the process of adding this flexibility, efficiency in making precise predictions is lost. Properly extended, economic theory can, of course, explain everything, but this is familiarly equivalent to saying that it predicts nothing.

My own prejudices, no doubt apparent from my own work, suggest that economic theory may be extended somewhat differently. My preferred approach is one of holding onto the predictive power provided by *homo economicus* while moving beyond the market relationship strictly defined. As the predictive power of this central motivational assumption is progressively weakened as we shift further from the simple exchange interaction, we should forthrightly acknowledge the limits of our science.

In practice, of course, the difference between the approach that I have here associated with Alchian and my own becomes minimal. When my purpose is didactic, I am quite willing to fall back on the extended utility function or transactions costs to assist me in explanation. And when Alchian's purpose is policy-oriented, he is quite willing to talk about one set of property rights as being more likely to produce desirable results than another. Indeed, his whole interest in property rights and institutional arrangements would be difficult to explain were it not for the fact that Professor Alchian does, implicitly perhaps, adopt his own version of *homo economicus*.

4

General Implications of Subjectivism in Economics

I have often argued that the "Austrians" seem, somehow, to be more successful in conveying the central principle of economics to students than alternative schools, enclaves or approaches. This theme has involved two components. First, I have argued that our most important social role is that of teaching students rather than that of serving as surrogate social engineers. Second, my hypothesis depended, of course, on a definition of just what the most important central principle in economics is. And my position is on record in this respect. *The* principle that exposure to economics *should* convey is that of the spontaneous coordination which the market achieves. The central principle of economics is not the economizing process; it is not the maximization of objective functions subject to constraints. Once we become methodologically trapped in the maximization paradigm, economics becomes applied mathematics or engineering.

This chapter was initially presented as a lecture at a conference on subjectivist economics, Dallas, Texas, December 1976.

In this connection, let me tell you a story. I recently talked with a prominent economist who mentioned that one of his colleagues had reported having several conversations with the then presidential candidate Jimmy Carter. This colleague passed along his view that Carter was a "good systems analyst," and my friend added, more or less as an afterthought, and "hence, a good economist." I very quickly and very emphatically put him straight, saying that nothing could be further from the "economic point of view," properly interpreted, than that of the systems analyst. Indeed this is precisely my own fear about Carter, that he is, in fact, a good systems analyst without the remotest understanding of the principle of spontaneous order. I should add here that, to my friend's credit, when I pointed this out to him, he immediately took my distinction as relevant. But it is, I think, a mark of how far our whole discipline has deteriorated when we slip so readily and naturally into the simple maximization paradigm.

Or perhaps "economists" should stay in that paradigm. Argument could be made to this effect on etymological grounds. Perhaps what I should be suggesting here is that we need to be studying and promulgating something other than "economics."

But enough of general methodology, although I shall not get very far away from it anywhere. To return to "subjectivist economics" more specifically, my hypothesis is that this sort of economic theory must further a better understanding of the principle of spontaneous coordination. But I need to support this hypothesis by convincing argument. Why does the subjectivist more readily learn and accept the principle of spontaneous order than the objectivist? He does so because that which he seeks to explain and to understand is different. The subjectivist is not trying to explain, positively or normatively, the allocation of scarce resources among uses; nor is his subject matter best described as *price* theory. What he is trying to explain is exchange, conceived in its broadest sense. His is a "theory of exchange," as I have repeatedly argued, but a theory of exchange of whatever it is that persons value. The positive aspects of the theory take form in predictions about the properties of equilibrium positions, potentially observable behaviorally through the cessation of trade among parties. He also predicts, again positively, that interferences with trade or exchange must create trading opportunities that remain unconsummated, and that the existence of such opportunities must necessarily be reflected in enforcement and policing problems. The subjectivist is not likely to accept what is perhaps the most sophisticated fallacy in economic theory, the notion that because certain relationships hold in equilibrium the forced interferences designed to implement these relationships will, in fact, be desirable. In such examples of this fallacy as "equal pay for equal work," even one of the stars in the subjectivist firmament, Professor Hayek, lost his way.

But let me be clear, and fair. I am not setting up some imaginary straw creature, labeled objectivist economics, for the purpose of saying that its subject matter necessarily and certainly leads to ignorance, bewilderment, and confusion, and that the subjectivist possesses the only key to wisdom. (I could expand on this a bit. It seems to me that one of the dangers of the subjectivist approach, and particularly in its pure Austrian variant, is the tendency to form a priesthood, with the converted talking only to those who are converts, and with the deliberate withdrawal from free and open espousal of subjectivist notions to the world around.) An understanding and appreciation of the principle of spontaneous order or coordination may emerge from the very citadels of objectivisim, and often does. After all, Adam Smith was no subjectivist. What I am implying is that to the extent that subjectivism tends to concentrate attention on the interaction among persons and away from the "economic problem," an understanding of the principle of order is facilitated rather than retarded. The post-Robbins maximizer must learn the principle of order in spite of rather than because of his analytical paradigm.

At this point I should restore Professor Hayek to his proper place in my overall league tables by endorsing his criticism of "scientism," a criticism also advanced by my own professor, Frank Knight. Hayek and Knight were sharply critical of any attempts to convert economics into a discipline analogous to a natural science. Economics is, or can be, scientific in a sense that is, I think, unique. The principle of spontaneous order is a scientific principle, in that it can be readily divorced from normative content. Unless we stay within the exchange paradigm, however, we lose the legitimately scientific principle and, instead, launch off into the scientistic implications that emerge directly from the maximization paradigm. Economists find themselves measuring social costs and social benefits, along with a little of everything else.

And, of course, to the extent that quantities may be measured, independently of choice behavior and hence objectively, there must exist an objectively determinate "solution" to any problem that is posed. There is some "optimal" allocation of economic resources, defined by the physical units of resource located in time and space. And let us recall here that Professor Tjallings Koopmans won a Nobel Prize in economics, not in engineering. He did so for his efforts that commenced from working out the optimal allocation of a set of tankers plying oil across the Atlantic during World War II, where the variables were ships, distances, port locations, barrels of oil, and, of course, a set of shadow prices. (To claim a bit of credit for myself here, I think I was a confirmed subjectivist long before I realized what I was because I recall thinking in 1946, when Koopmans was lecturing on this at the University of Chicago, that there seemed to be absolutely no economic content in what he was doing, at least as I then, and now, conceived our proper subject matter to be.) There must also exist an equilibrium set of prices that are objectively computable, at least conceptually, and indeed, we have observed Professor Herbert Scarf of Yale now trying to work out ways of computing equilibrium prices, which effort seems, to the subjectivist, an absurd exercise.

To the extent that there exist objectively determinate and physically describable allocations or imputations that may be evaluated by some efficiency or optimization criterion, the market is necessarily reduced to one among several institutional devices whose operations may be compared one with another. The market becomes an "analogue computing device," a "mechanism," which may or may not rank better than its alternatives in terms of the objectifiable performance criteria. At this level, the distinction between the market and the centrally planned economy is purely in comparative performance. And, at this point, there is a subtle but vitally important principle or insight that the objectivist tends to neglect. Economic performance can only be conceived in values; but how are values determined? By prices, but prices emerge only in markets. They have no meaning in a non-market context. Hence, the market can hardly be compared in terms of performance against a nonmarket institution. In this sense, the whole efficiency criterion as traditionally applied to socialist economies, even as idealized, is devoid of meaning.

The 1930s debate between Mises on the one hand and Lange, Lerner and Dickinson on the other was never properly grounded. As this debate has been widely interpreted, the conceptual possibility of market socialism was made dependent on the informational potential of the central planning authority, a problem that an iterative procedure was alleged to resolve. But this is not the central issue. As I tried to discuss in my little book *Cost and Choice*,[1] the issue is not simply one of information. The central issue is the critical interdependence between market choice itself and the informational content of this process which can only be revealed as the process is allowed to occur. Let me try to explain by an example. This seems to me to be a vitally important point, but it is one that I am not at all sure how to present here. Suppose that we consider an allocation of apples and oranges between two persons, A and B, persons who are located externally to us, say, in Timbuktu. If we know their utility functions, along with the initial endowments of the two commodities, we can define the "efficient allocation" of apples and oranges, an allocation that would, of course, be equivalent to that which

---

[1] *Cost and Choice: An Inquiry in Economic Theory* (Chicago: Markham Publishing Co., 1969).

would be attained as a result of voluntary exchange or trade between A and B. But we cannot, as external observers, possibly know the utility functions because such functions do not, and cannot, exist independently of the choice action of A and B in the exchange process itself. That is to say, even if we could establish perfect verbal communication with A and B, they could not "write down" their utility functions in any meaningful operational sense. We may, if we desire, postulate utility functions for the two persons, as given to us or as imagined for them, and we may then define efficiency by these postulated functions. But this would amount to empty exercise since there would be little or no relationship to the efficiency, so defined, and that which an actual exchange process might generate. (Although I cannot go into it here, there is an affinity between my criticism of orthodox procedures in economic theory and the radical Marxist-oriented criticism, by Gintis and others, centered on the assumption of invariant preferences.)

Considerations such as those outlined in the example here have led my colleague Robert Staaf to despair of even using indifference-curve analytics. I do not go quite so far, but I can recognize the pedagogical problem. Utility-function, indifference-curve constructions may be useful in depicting or illustrating the underlying rationality of the voluntary exchange process, provided that these constructions are understood in strictly subjective terms, as constructions that cannot, in their nature, be communicated to observers independently of the exchange process within which they emerge.

In one sense, it becomes misleading at the outset to say that persons "act as if they were maximizing a utility function subject to constraints," since this terminology itself

tends to suggest that the utility functions exist independently of the acting-choosing process. It is better, at this
level of discussion, to say simply that persons choose among
alternatives as they arise, and that there is, hopefully,
enough consistency in their behavior to allow us to make
some predictions about changes in outcomes as a result of
changes in the choice alternatives. At this point, the strict
Austrians may enter into a debate with me and, more important, with those who insist on the empirical corroboration
of the elementary principles of human behavior in voluntary exchange processes. Such debate has always seemed to
me to be of only indirect significance. As Frank Knight
used to say, most of the empirical work in economics is
"proving water runs downhill," a proposition that the Austrians would scarcely question.

Indirectly, however, and in opportunity-cost terms, the
empirical-nonempirical debate is of importance. The young
and aspiring economist who becomes the expert empiricist
has necessarily sacrificed training time in learning more
about the process to which his highly polished technical
tools are to be applied. These gaps in the training of modern
economists are beginning to show up in many forms, not the
least of which is the deadly dullness that dominates whole
departments in many universities and colleges.

I should like to say something about the relationship between subjectivist economics and mathematical economics.
The important and central principle that the subjectivist
paradigm advances is that of spontaneous order, as I have
already suggested several times. The theoretical foundations here can be readily mathematized. But the mathematics called for is not the maximization of objective functions
subject to constraints. The mathematically inclined econo-

mist who seeks to put all analysis into this form is already on the wrong track, and he is likely to confuse both himself and his students. The mathematics dictated here is that of general equilibrium, properly understood, the search for the solutions of systems of simultaneous equations, solutions that emerge from the interdependence among the variables described in the whole system of equations. For this reason, I find no difficulty at all in allowing the general equilibrium theorist to do his work alongside his subjectivist, nonmathematical counterpart, provided that he does not slip into error by somehow imputing, even at some conceptual level, objective meaning into his wholly imaginary constructs.

I am perhaps even more favorable toward the sort of thinking that game theory fosters, and especially in its development of solution concepts applicable to many-person games. Almost by necessity, the game theorist is led to think about an interaction process that produces an outcome through the behavior of many participants, each one of whom acts independently of the others. Game theory takes the wrong turn, however, to the extent that the emphasis shifts to the normative problem of defining optimal strategies for particular players or coalitions of players, even for games against nature and even for the all-inclusive coalition.

I have suggested that the principle of spontaneous order is "scientific" in the sense that it embodies a logically coherent argument. But does the economist who considers his main role to be that of teaching this principle to his students necessarily plead guilty to the charge that he is imposing an ideology? In one sense the answer is yes. Adam Smith was offering an alternative vision of how an economy might work. It was necessary to provide this alternative vision before the mercantilist blinders could be removed. Smith's effort was, in this quite literal sense, subversive of the existing order and of the set of attitudes that supported this order. I see no reason why our task in 1976 is any different from that in 1776. We must offer a vision of economic process that is not natural to man's ordinary ways of thinking. And faith in the efficacy of the process of spontaneous coordination arises only from a thorough understanding which only economists are equipped to transmit.

Milton Friedman, a friend whose work I admire greatly, objects to the Austrian-subjectivist approach largely on the grounds that it implies conversion rather than gradual conviction by the weight of logical argument and empirical tests. In part, this objection is based on the observable priesthood tendencies, which I noted above. More important, however, Friedman's objection seems to be based on what I regard as a naive notion of how persons shift paradigms. Admittedly, a connection between accumulated empirical evidence and paradigm shifts must exist, but this is not nearly so direct as Friedman seems to think. But I think we all must admit that the patterns are mysterious here, and these may well vary considerably from one person to another. For my own part, I do not object to the "preaching" implications of subjectivist economics, although I can appreciate both the dangers of this and the advantages of something like the Friedman position.

Unfortunately, most modern economists have no idea of what they are doing or even of what they are ideally supposed to be doing. I challenge any of you to take any issue of any economics journal and convince yourself, and me, that a randomly chosen paper will have a social productivity greater than zero. Most modern economists are simply doing what other economists are doing while living off a form of dole that will simply not stand critical scrutiny. Beware the day for educators generally when the taxpaying public finds out that the king really has no clothes.

I think I know what I am doing, and I think that most of those who espouse a variant of Austrian subjectivist economics know what they are doing. And I think that our efforts are socially productive, highly so. I suppose that all of this finally reduces to an admonition to keep the faith, whether we want to call this doing economics, subjectivist economics, Austrian economics, or something else. The set of ideas and attitudes that emerges from an understanding of the principle of spontaneous order can be transmitted. We can have a part to play in developing a meaningful "public philosophy," even if this amounts to little more now than playing the role of subversives of the dominating mindset that conceives the economy as chaos independent of collective controls. But recall two things. Adam Smith had no idea that he would, in fact, work a revolution in economic thinking and in economic policy in the half-century after 1776. And the same Adam Smith memorably observed: "There's a deal of ruin in a nation." Keep the faith.

5

Natural and Artifactual Man

I claim no competence in ethology, and I am fully aware
that there are numerous attributes that have been adduced to make the categorical distinction between the human and higher animal species, attributes such as language,
sense of death, ability to think in complex fashion, etc. I
want to concentrate here on a single attribute that does
make men categorically different from even the higher
animals, an attribute that seems to me to be too much
neglected in modern economics.

We know that we could examine the behavior of my dog
scientifically. We could set up experiments, and we could, I
am sure, derive a utility function from such experiments,
much as the economists who work with rats have done at
Texas A & M. This exercise might be useful in many respects. On the basis of the utility function so derived, we
might be able to predict with reasonable accuracy just how
my dog would behave if his opportunity set were modified
in various ways. This accuracy in prediction could be in-

This chapter was initially presented as a lecture at a Liberty Fund
Series Conference in Blacksburg, Virginia, in July 1978.

creased if we extended the experiment, and the predictions, to apply to a large-number, or representative, setting rather than to a single behaving unit.

How would this procedure differ if we experimented with and made predictions about man, either as individual men and women, or as representative members of a large group? Once I pose the issue in this way, the response, and my emphasis here, should be evident to you. Our predictions about man must always be less accurate than our predictions about animals. But why is this so? What does man do that animals do not do? Clearly, the standard attributes called upon to categorize man differently from his fellow mammals will help us little here. We need to do better than this; man does not become less predictable because he uses language.

What I am getting at is that a central difference between my dog and any one of us lies in his lack of any sense of becoming different from what he is. This is to be contrasted with your sense of "becoming" as a central part, indeed probably the most important part, of life itself. As human beings, we know that we are going to die; perhaps my dog does not know this about himself. But we, as human beings, also know that we can, within limits, shape the form of being that we shall be between now and the time of death, even when we fully reckon on the stochastic pattern of life expectancy.

For my purposes, I shall call my dog a "natural" animal, and I shall call any one of us a "natural and artifactual" animal, or, perhaps preferably, an artifactual animal bounded by natural constraints. We are, and will be, at least in part, that which we make ourselves to be. We construct our own beings, again within limits. We are artifactual, as much like the pottery sherds that the archaeologists dig up as like the animals whose fossils they also find.

A digression is necessary at this point in order to forestall possible misunderstanding. My title, and my general discussion in terms of the dichotomy between "natural" and "artifactual" man, does not imply that I equate "natural" wholly with biological or genetic elements. I accept the importance of what Hayek calls the "culturally evolved man," which, in a sense, is neither "natural" nor "artifactual." For my purposes, to the extent that individuals are rigidly bound by culturally evolved rules of conduct or modes of behavior, these elements would make up part of "natural man," or, better stated, "nonartifactual man." On the other hand, to the extent that culturally evolved rules of conduct exist but require an act of choice by persons to accept or to reject adherence, these elements of behavior would be artifactual, in my terminology here. My emphasis is concentrated on the simple distinction between that part of man's behavior that is "programmed," and hence "predictable scientifically," and that which is not.

There is, of course, nothing new or even novel in what I am saying here, and you should have no difficulty in accepting my statements. But I am trying to develop this argument for a purpose, which is one of demonstrating that modern economic theory forces upon us patterns of thought that make elementary recognition of the whole "becoming" part of our behavior very difficult to analyze and easy to neglect.

Let me begin by offering a brief and only partial catalog of what I think are misleading directions. First, consider human capital theory. I do not deny the productivity of in-

sights gained by looking at education and training as investment in human capital, nor do I reject out of hand the
usefulness of attempts to measure rates of return on such
investment along with comparisons of rates on ordinary
investment outlays. As you know, the human capital approach has been criticized, by Jack Wiseman among others,
because it tends to neglect the direct consumption attributes
of the apparent investment process, and notably in education. I have no quarrel with such criticism, but it is quite
different from what I want to advance here. A good part of
education can be modeled appropriately neither as capital
investment nor as consumption of final services. Instead it
must somehow be modeled as "spending on becoming"—
on becoming the person that we want to be rather than the
one we think we might be if the spending is not made in
this way. (This purpose of education is, of course, clear
when we think of education for children as determined by
parents and by society rather than by the children themselves. We do not educate children primarily to produce
income streams or even utility streams; we educate them to
make them over into persons "better" than and different
from those they would be without the educational process.
At least this is our intent.) But let me return to self-"investment." The activity is investment in a sense because life
through time is reckoned. But it is not investment in any
life-cycle sense, which might be deemed akin to that of the
squirrel that accumulates nuts for winter, yet with no conception of itself as something other than the squirrel it is
and will remain. I am not proposing to deny that there is a
lot of squirrel in each of us, to our credit perhaps. I am,
instead, saying that there is much more to apparent "invest-

ment behavior" (defined as nonconsumption) than squirreling. (And I should add more to it than the Ricardian extension of the life-cycle model to intergenerational linkages.)

The metaphor of "capital" investment seems misplaced when we think of a person's outlay of time and money on information, on knowledge. A person is not investing with the aim or purpose of increasing the size of an objectively measured income stream in perpetuity, a stream that may be converted or potentially converted into consumption by the selfsame person or his heirs. He is investing in becoming the different person that he must become as he acquires knowledge and wisdom; he cannot do otherwise than become different. And as he does so, he must embody a different "utility function," if we choose to carry around this baggage of the economist with us. Hence, he must choose differently if he should be confronted with the same constraints as before, which is in itself a logical impossibility because of the nature of time itself. As you can see, even to talk about present values of future income streams, about rates of return, is of questionable worth in analyzing such behavior as I am trying to identify here.

As a second example, let us consider the Stigler-Becker proposition to the effect that economists should proceed on the assumption that utility functions are stable through time and invariant as among persons.[1] Introspectively and observationally, we may want to reject this notion out of hand. But my interest does not lie in the empirical validity or invalidity of the invariance assumption itself. Instead, my

---

[1] George J. Stigler and Gary S. Becker, "De Gustibus Non Est Disputandum," *American Economic Review* 67, no. 2 (March 1977): 76–90.

interest lies in the thought pattern or mind-set that the Stigler-Becker hypothesis imposes on anyone who tries to analyze behavior seriously.

Consider their own example of music and music appreciation. The individual's preference function, which is unchanging, contains music as a basic component. Music now is produced by current inputs and time, and music in future periods is, in part, produced by current-period investment in music appreciation and in time spent on current consumption. Hence, music becomes cheaper to produce relative to other consumption or end items as time progresses; a person is, therefore, predicted to purchase more inputs to produce music as costs fall. There is no need to resort to the notion that tastes or preferences have shifted.

But what does this approach imply with respect to the basic commodity or service in the preference function, music? There is no change possible in the *quality* of the service purchased in their model; music appreciation cannot induce a shift from rock to classical, yet is this not precisely what we should expect to observe? It seems impossible, in the Stigler-Becker world, to invest in becoming more appreciative of music or of anything else. This restriction tends to shut off or to foreclose whole aspects of behavior from analysis and examination.

My purpose, however, is not to criticize particular areas of concentration, but to advance a broad criticism against economic theory generally. If I may resort to philosophical terms, what I am objecting to in modern economic theory is its *teleological* foundations, its tendency to force all analyzable behavior into the straitjacket of "maximizing a utility or objective function under constraints." In one way, I am suggesting that the utilitarian origins of nineteenth-century political economy may have come to haunt us and to do us great damage.

Let me try to put my argument positively. It is useful to think of man as an imagining being, which in itself sets him apart from other species. A person sees himself or herself in many roles, capacities, and natures, in many settings, in many times, in many places. As one contemplates moving from imagination to potential behavior, however, constraints emerge to bound or limit the set of prospects severely. One might, for example, imagine himself living in any age of history, past or imagined future. But as action is approached, the constraint of the here and now impinges. One imagines an ability to fly unaided through space, to walk on water, to live on love. But one faces up to the reality of the limits imposed by the laws of science before the real replaces the romantic. One can imagine himself to be of the opposite sex until the physical structure of his own body is allowed to intervene. One can think of what he might have been with different sets of genes.

Once all of the possible constraints are accounted for (historical, geographic, cultural, physical, genetic, sexual), there still remains a large set of possible persons that one might imagine himself to be, or might imagine himself capable of becoming. There is room for "improvement," for the construction of what might be. Further, in thinking about realizable prospects, a person is able to rank these in some fashion, to classify members of the set as "better" or "worse."

Constrained by the several "natural" limits (which, as noted above, include the cultural), an individual is further constrained by his own construction of himself in past periods. But recognizing the possible prospects that remain open to him through his remaining life span, and ranking these prospects in some way, the individual remains capable of achieving the prospect that he chooses. To make such choice, the costs of the alternatives must be reckoned along with the anticipated benefits. But here I lapse too closely into standard economists' terminology, which is precisely the trap I want to avoid in this lecture, I should emphasize that the relationships between the prospects that might be achieved and the costs of achieving these may not be at all clear, indeed they could not be.

Nonetheless, the prospects of becoming are sufficient to channel action, to divert resources away from the automatic routine that utility maximization, as normally presented, seems to embody. And choices made in becoming a different person are irrevocable, regardless of their productivity, when viewed *ex post*. We move through time, constructing ourselves as artifactual persons. We are not, and cannot be, the "same person" in any utility-maximization sense. There is nothing in personal behavior akin to Adam Smith's "discipline of continuous dealings" to enable us to undo or to correct past sins of omission or commission.

Much of what I have said to this point is probably broadly acceptable to you, at least as warning against pushing our formalizations in economics too far. I have done little more than stress what Frank Knight spent much time discussing, namely, man's tendency to want to want better things, to become a better man. This theme is fully developed in the essay "Ethics and the Economic Interpretation," the first essay in *The Ethics of Competition*.[2] More recently, Burt

---

[2] Chicago: Midway Reprint, 1967, pp. 19–40.

Weisbrod[3] has explicitly discussed the possibility of investment in securing "better" sets of utility functions. What I have done is to marry this discussion of man's desire to modify his own being, with what may be called a subjective or even neo-Austrian theory of time and choice. In the latter, I have been influenced by G. L. S. Shackle, whose difficult but idea-packed book *Epistemics and Economics*[4] I have been struggling to get through this summer. I have also had access to Shackle's 1976 Keynes lecture to the British academy, "Time and Choice."[5] Further, I have had occasion to read Jack Wiseman's paper, "Costs and Decisions."[6] You will also recognize that much of my discussion of choice in this paper is related to my earlier treatment in *Cost and Choice*.[7] To the philosophical cognoscenti, much of my discussion probably embodies the influence of Whitehead, albeit indirectly since I had never read Whitehead before completing the draft of this lecture.

We could, I suspect, have an interesting discussion if I stopped at this point. But there is more to my purpose than merely to raise some of the issues of general approach or method. I want to argue that our failure to allow for any accounting of the sort of choice behavior involving investment in becoming something different has inhibited our

---

[3] Burt Weisbrod, "Comparing Utility Functions in Efficiency Terms or, What Kind of Utility Functions Do We Want?" *American Economic Review* 67, no. 5 (December 1977): 991–95.

[4] Cambridge: At the University Press, 1972.

[5] G. L. S. Shackle, "Time and Choice," *Proceedings of the British Academy* 62 (1976): 306–29.

[6] Mimeographed (University of York, 1978).

[7] Chicago: Markham Publishing Co., 1969.

ability to understand as well as our willingness to try to understand some of the problems of our time, both individual and social. By implicitly refusing to consider man as artifactual, we neglect the "constitution of private man," which roughly translates as "character," as well as the "constitution of public men," which translates into the necessary underpinning of a free society, the "character" of society, if you will.

Let me take care at this point not to be misunderstood. I am not calling for the return of some romantic image of man that transcends "human nature," an image of man that you and I cannot even recognize as our fellow in plausibly imagined social order. I am not calling for some idealized person who might be imagined independently of the very real constraints of "natural man." I have used the term *artifactual* here precisely for the purpose of allowing some recognition of the basic constraints of human nature while, at the same time, allowing for wide areas of choice within these constraints, areas within which we can, and do, construct ourselves as individuals, from the base largely constructed for us by our forebears. Artifactual man, along with his institutions of social order, was embodied in the wisdom of the eighteenth century, a wisdom that modern man has seemed in danger of losing altogether.

How can the prevailing orthodoxy account for such a simple act as that by a person in quitting smoking, an example that was discussed at some length by Tom Schelling[8] at the New York meetings? Or going on a diet? If the

---

[8] T. Schelling, "Altruism, Meanness, and Other Potentially Strategic Behaviors," *American Economic Review* 68, no. 2 (May 1978): 229–30.

person's utility function is unchanged, and if the constraints faced do not change, how can we account for such behavior?

The explanation falls into place readily if we allow for some recognition that persons imagine themselves to be other than they are and that they take action designed to achieve imagined states of being. A smoker can surely imagine himself or herself freed of the habit, with a transformed set of preferences that would not include any desire to smoke. Reckoning on such a prospect as within the realm of the possible, a person sacrifices current enjoyment in the uncertain quest for the state of being that he can imagine. A person may undertake such renunciatory behavior voluntarily and spontaneously through a whole sequence of periods, or such behavior may take the form of the adoption of some quasi-permanent rule that will effectively impose constraints on predicted lapses into the satisfaction of "natural" desires. A smoker may carry cigarettes with him and face up to the temptation of his desires each and every time that these arise. Or a smoker may throw out all of his cigarette inventory and impose upon himself a strict rule against further purchases. Or, he may even go much further and authorize others to coerce him against indulgence of his desires.

As the smoker abstains, or as he is forced to abstain by the operation of an internal or an external constraint, he will find that he does become different from the person that he was. His preferences shift; he becomes the nonsmoker that he had imagined himself capable of becoming. The costs of having achieved such a transformation, when viewed *ex post,* may seem to have been trivial or even nonexistent, whereas the benefits may seem immense. But how could these costs and benefits, measured *ex post,* be of value in informing the calculus of the "other" person at the stage of the initial decision?

This example of the smoker is simple and straightforward, but I should emphasize its generality in the context of this paper. The behavior examined is not restricted to addicting goods and services, as some critics might immediately suggest. Almost the same analysis can be applied to any aspect of human behavior that represents "civility" in the larger meaning of this term. I refer here inclusively to manners, etiquette, codes of conduct, standards of decorum, and, most important, morals. A person conducts himself, within the natural limits available to him, and the artifactual person he becomes does, at any moment, maximize utility subject to constraints. But constraints on his own behavior imposed in past periods have shaped the form of his utility function, perhaps out of all recognition in some primitivistic sense. I may cite Frank Knight at this point. From the longer excerpt that George Stigler put on his calendar, I cite only the following: "Insofar as man is wise or good, his 'character' is acquired chiefly by posing as better than he is, until a part of his pretense becomes a habit."[9]

I cannot fully articulate my worries to the effect that modern economic theory leads us away from any appreciation of artifactual man, but I was highly sympathetic to a statement made by C. W. Griffin in a letter to *Business Week* in response to an earlier article on the intrusion of genetics into economics. Griffin said: "From the naively optimistic eighteenth-century view of man as a potentially

---

[9] Frank Knight, "The Planful Act: The Possibilities and Limitations of Collective Rationality," in *Freedom and Reform* (New York and London: Harper & Brothers, 1947).

rational God, we have plunged to the naively pessimistic extreme of viewing man as an individual ant."[10]

We find statements everywhere to the effect that modern man has lost the faith in progress that was pervasive in the post-Enlightenment period, the eighteenth and nineteenth centuries, and most of this century. J. B. Bury entitled his classic little book *The Idea of Progress,*[11] implying by this title that the idea may be more important than the reality. This implication is surely correct in the normative sense of exerting influences on behavior. The hopes for man, individually and collectively, held out by the post-Enlightenment social philosophers may have been naive, especially when viewed from the perspective of our age. But the lesson to be drawn is surely and emphatically not one of resignation to man's fate as a natural animal.

We shall indeed revert to the jungle if we continue on our present course, whether in our private behavior patterns, or in our collective-governmental-institutional dynamic, aided and abetted by the make-work of the so-called social sciences. If we twiddle around with our "scientistic" economics and political science, if we remain so enraptured by esoteric puzzles, if we place exclusive faith in empirical demonstrations or in evolutionary processes, we are contributing to the process of deterioration.

Individually, persons must recapture an ability to imagine themselves capable of becoming "better" persons than they are. But the ranking of prospects requires valuation. "Pushpin is not as good as poetry." The role of education is to provide persons with both an array of imagined prospects

---

[10] May 8, 1978, p. 6.
[11] New York: Dover Publications, 1932.

and some means of valuation. Modern education is, as we know, failing dismally in both parts of this role, but perhaps more seriously in the second than in the first. There is little or no transmission of the cultural-value heritage of the historically imagined American dream in which individuals were able to hold out images of themselves and their society in accordance with generally accepted standards of "betterness." We could, of course, discuss such matters at length, but my emphasis in this paper is on other aspects of the modern dilemma. In particular, I want to concentrate on the role that political economists might play in promoting rather than holding back the good society of free and responsible men and women, a society that we all should seek. By general agreement, the economist has little or no business teaching morals or ethics, and no justification for building his theories on romantic notions of man that will not stand empirical test.

Lest I should become too confused, and become too confusing to you in the process, let me begin at the beginning, and tell you what prompted this whole effort. I did not set out with any intent of preparing a general methodological disquisition. But I was led to the sort of inquiry that my early remarks suggest by an attempt to explain satisfactorily to myself just why attitudes that seem so natural to me seem so difficult for others. Note carefully that I refer to "attitudes" here, not to ideas. In particular, I sought to understand why the "constitutional attitude" seems so foreign to so many of my fellow economists, to understand why this central aspect of what was a part of the conventional wisdom of our Founding Fathers now seems so elusive. My usage of the word *artifactual* is borrowed directly from Vincent Ostrom, who has repeatedly emphasized the necessity of considering the political constitution as an artifact, to be categorically distinguished from an evolved legal order.[12] The American experience, perhaps unique in history, has embodied the attitude that we *create* the institutions within which we interact, one with another, that we construct the rules that define the game that we all must play. But we can never lose sight of the elementary fact that the selection of the rules, "constitutional choice," is of a different attitudinal dimension from the selection of strategies within defined rules.

I was led to ask, however, whether persons who do not and cannot conceive themselves to be artifactual (even if, in fact, they are and must be), can easily conceive of artifactual social institutions, artifactual rules of the game, to be chosen apart from the simple selection of strategies to be played in the complex interaction process defined by the rules of order. Does the manner in which men model their own behavior affect, and perhaps profoundly, the way that they model the social institutions under which they live? If individuals conceive themselves in the teleological image of modern economics, can they shift gears to a nonteleological image of a community?

We know that the utilitarians were unable to make this leap, at least consistently and without much ambiguity and confusion, which plagues us still. We know also that modern economics has become more, not less, teleological. In the post-Robbins era, we define our subject matter as the study of the allocation of scarce means among alternative ends, and the idea of maximization under constraints becomes

---

[12] See his "David Hume as a Political Analyst," mimeographed (Indiana University, 1976).

central to all that we do. In the wake of methodological consensus, the theoretical welfare economists, having been forced to abandon naive utilitarianism, played teasingly with the Pareto criterion (which is not at all teleological, at least in the way that I interpret it), only to abandon this in favor of the "social welfare function." In so doing, they were explicitly extending the teleological model of the individual maximizer to that for the community or collectivity as a unit. To those economists who made such an extension, Arrow's impossibility theorem was a genuinely shocking revelation. A "social welfare function" must be constructed in order to allow for some modeling of the collectivity in teleological terms, but such a function becomes a logical impossibility under plausible conditions. What to do? What to do? I need not say that the welfare economists, among whom I should surely include Kenneth Arrow himself, are, to this day, groping for answers.

As you can recognize I am on familiar territory here, but partial corroboration for much of my argument lies in the chilling neglect of my own attempts, over a quarter-century, to secure general acknowledgment that no problem exists. Why should anyone have ever tried to model a community of *separate* persons teleologically, as if somehow "social states" could be, or should be, arrayed in some order of ascendancy, in terms of a single maximand? To me, as I stated in 1954,[13] such an effort has seemed misguided from the outset, even absurd. But why do most of my colleagues persist in their efforts? What is the difference between me and them?

---

[13] James M. Buchanan, "Social Choice in Voting and the Market," *Journal of Political Economy* 62 (August 1954): 334–43.

These questions are in the background of my exploratory remarks in this lecture (the appropriate place to be exploratory). Perhaps we should have been examining more closely the models for individual choice, and the images conveyed in those models, rather than unduly concentrating attention on the amalgamation of separate individual choices into collective results. Perhaps the nonteleological elements of individual choice have been too much neglected by us all. If each one of us is defined by an unchanging and invariant utility function, the Benthamite challenge remains ever present. Conceptually, the adding-up problem beckons, and this objective, once achieved, leads us back to the implied authoritarianism of Bentham's progeny, the practicing social democrats of our time.

But what happens to this progression once we so much as recognize that individuals do not maximize anything that remains stable for more than the logical moment for analysis. The maximization calculus may remain highly useful as a logic of choice, but only to the extent that its severe limits are explicitly acknowledged. Heraclitus noted that man does not step into the same river twice, first, because the stream has passed, and, second, because man too has moved forward in time. Choice is, and must be, irrevocable, and a person is constructed by the choices he has made sequentially through time, within the natural and the artifactual constraints that have limited his possibilities. The rational ideal eliminates choice, as Shackle emphasizes. Choice requires the presence of uncertainty for its very meaning. But choice also implies a moral responsibility for action. To rationalize or to explain choices in terms of either genetic endowments or social environment removes the elements of freedom and of responsibility. "Natural man," in the model of some behavioral responder to stimuli, akin to my dog, contradicts both the notion of individual liberty and that of individual responsibility for the consequences of the choices made. Man must bear the responsibilities for his own choices because of his artifactual nature, because he has available to him alternative "choosables," to use Shackle's term, because man makes his own history.

If individual man is to be free, he is to be held accountable, he is to be deemed responsible for his actions. But at the same time he is allowed to take credit for his achievement. Who can claim credit for results that could have been predicted from nature? From a knowledge of his genetic endowment or his social environment, or both? But once man is conceived in the image of an artifact, who constructs himself through his own choices, he sheds the animalistically determined path of existence laid out for him by the orthodox economists' model. A determined and programmed existence is replaced by the uncertain and exciting quest that life must be.

If man can envisage himself as a product of his own making, as embodying prospects for changing himself into one of the imagined possibilities that he might be, it becomes relatively easy for him to envisage changing the basic rules of social order in the direction of imagined good societies. In doing so, however, nothing teleological can be introduced since man must recognize that even within his own private sphere of action there is no maximand. Individually, man invests in becoming that which he is not. Collectively, men agree to modify the artifactual rules within which they interact one with another so as to allow individualized pursuit of whatever men may choose.

A felicific calculus becomes absurd in this setting, as

does all talk of such things as "national goals," "national priorities," or even such familiar things as "university objectives." Traditionally, many of us who have been critical of such talk remark that "only individuals can have goals." But I am here advancing the more radical notion that *not even* individuals have well-defined and well-articulated objectives that exist independently of choices themselves. Introspectively, we must realize that we do not. My plea is that we begin to temper our analytical-explanatory thought patterns to allow for what we know to be real, regardless of the havoc wrought to our aesthetically appealing logical structures.

Out of all this there emerges a strong defense of individual liberty that cannot readily be advanced by the modern economist, influenced as he is by his utilitarian heritage. The modern economist can introduce time into his models only if he treats individuals as squirrels, to return to my earlier example. The squirrel's behavior can be interpreted as maximizing the present value of his utility stream. Given his constraints, and his utility function, the squirrel is not, and cannot be, concerned with the size of his "choice" set, with the existence or nonexistence of his rejected alternatives. A dramatically different attitude emerges, however, in the conception of the artifactual man that I have sketched out here. A person chooses, as Shackle stresses, from among many imagined futures, and he remains necessarily uncertain as to how that which he chooses will work out. He has a clear interest in seeing that the choice set, the set of alternative imagined futures, remains as open as is naturally possible, and, if constrained, that the constraints be also of his own choosing. The deliberate closing off of future options by the introduction of apparently irrelevant constraints, externally imposed, must damage the individual who knows that he must choose among uncertain prospects continually through time.

Consider, for example, an urban dweller who does not, in the orthodox analysis, embody an argument for privacy in his utility function. Within the corpus of formal analysis, such a person cannot be much concerned about the introduction of zoning restrictions that effectively force a higher concentration of persons in space. By contrast, consider the same urban dweller in the image suggested in this paper. He does not, and cannot, predict that person he may want to become in subsequent periods. He wants to "keep his options open," because he can imagine himself to be someone quite different from the person he now is. He does not, let us say, choose to leave the urban center today, tomorrow, or next week. But he can imagine himself becoming the person who could make a future choice to move to the suburbs or the country. He seeks to hold all such options open, even if his behavior, viewed in retrospect, indicates no exercise of the options in question. The building of the Berlin Wall harmed every person living in East Berlin. This is a simple statement of fact that orthodox economists would find difficult to interpret by means of their prevailing analytics.

Man wants liberty to become the man he wants to become. He does so precisely because he does not know what man he will want to become in time. Let us remove once and for all the instrumental defense of liberty, the only one that can possibly be derived directly from orthodox economic analysis. Man does not want liberty in order to maximize his utility, or that of the society of which he is a part. *He wants liberty to become the man he wants to become.*

Part Two

Economics as a
Social Science

6

Economics and Its Scientific Neighbors

There exists something that is called "economics." Courses in this something are offered in most universities; departmental faculties exist as separate administrative units. Specialized professional positions, in both private and public industry, are held by "economists." Professional journals and many books are written, printed, and presumably read, which libraries and bookshops catalog under economics. All of this creates the presumption that there is some widely shared common language, some special communication network among those who qualify as professionals, which makes for efficiency in discourse. Such a language is a necessary condition for science, but it is not a sufficient one. The efficiency in discourse must be measured also against the standards of science, which are those of understanding, not utility, of predictive ability, not platitudes, of objectively detached interpretation, not reasoned justification.

This chapter was initially published in *The Structure of Economic Science: Essays on Methodology*, ed. Sherman Roy Krupp (Englewood Cliffs, N.J.: Prentice-Hall, 1966), pp. 166–83. Permission to reprint is herewith acknowledged.

To an extent at least, "economics" qualifies as a science under these criteria. I propose to begin with this economics as empirical fact and to examine in some detail the relations of this science with its neighbors. Preliminary to the central questions it is useful to make some general observations about the development of economics itself. Insofar as one who is himself inside the discipline is able to discern movements in the whole, to me economics seems to be currently undergoing two apparently contradictory trend changes. The independence of economics in any broad disciplinary sense is rapidly breaking down, while, at the same time, specialization among the subdisciplines, within economics, is increasing apace.

Was economics ever so independent of its scientific neighbors as the bureaucracy of professional specialization makes it seem? Its subject matter emerged, scarcely a century ago, from "political economy," which, in its turn, sprang classical and full-blown from an earlier "moral philosophy." The scientific origins of economics lay hidden from their early expositors, and classical political economy was explicitly prejudiced toward reform. Its emphasis was on *improving* the institutions commanding its attention; *understanding* such institutions was always a secondary, even if necessary, purpose. Improvement did, as we know, materialize; the social transformation dictated by the classical precepts was, to an extent, realized.

The practical success of classical economics was responsible, in part, for its scientific undoing. The distinctions between scientific propositions and proposals for social reform were blurred from the outset. This led critics, who quite properly disputed classical prejudices toward social structure, to attack, and to appear to attack, the central propositions of the scientific analysis. This confusion has plagued economics and continues to plague it even now. The physical sciences have, by and large, escaped this confusion, and herein lies their prestige. Only in the recent discussions of the hydrogen bomb and radiation has there appeared anything akin to the elementary confusion between positive prediction and normative engineering that has pervaded economic discussion. Economists have, from the beginning of the discipline, been in the position faced by J. Robert Oppenheimer. And, they have, unfortunately for the science, chosen much as he seems to have done. As a result, the interests of economists have been rarely, if ever, wholly scientific, and, on occasion, have been explicitly ascientific. The personal inclination toward social involvement has proved too strong for most, even for those who shun the limelight and who remain, physically, within the ivoried towers. In this perspective, Pareto stands dominant over a narrowly confined group of lesser figures.

What Is Economics?

The science advanced, nonetheless, despite the noise generated by inconsequential argument, and there has been, and remains, content in the words *economics* and *economist*. Before the relationships among this science and its neighbors can be discussed, brief note of what this content is seems in order. What is the common language? What are the simple principles? How does one identify an economist?

By way of illustration, I propose to design here a simple conceptual experiment. One of the ancient Greek philosophers is credited with the statement: "Anything worth doing is worth doing well." As our conceptual experiment, let us suppose that we select a randomly drawn sample from the general population. We give each person in the sample the adage cited above, and we ask him to comment upon it. We then observe their comments and attempt some sort of classification.

No single test could, of course, possibly be wholly conclusive, but it seems quite possible that the simple experiment proposed here would, in fact, provide us with a rough and ready manner of classifying economists and distinguishing them from the general public of which they form a part. There would be, in other words, a characteristic economist's response to the adage which would not be shared by large numbers of other persons. Additional, and more discriminating tests could, of course, be devised which would further delineate the economists from the remaining community of scientists. But these need not be elaborated here since the single experiment is sufficient to illustrate the elemental principles of the science.

The economist's stock-in-trade—his tools—lies in his ability and his proclivity to think about all questions in terms of *alternatives*. The truth judgment of the moralist, which says that something is either wholly right or wholly wrong, is foreign to him. The win-lose, yes-no discussion of politics is not within his purview. He does not recognize the either-or, the all-or-nothing, situation as his own. His is not the world of the mutually exclusives. Instead, his is a world of adjustment, of coordinated conflict, of *mutual gains*. To the economist, there are, of course, many things worth doing that are not worth doing well since he is trained, professionally, to think in terms of a continuous scale of variation both in doing things and in criteria for judging them done well.

The theorems that are of relevance to the economist are

all constructed from this simple base. These may be germane to the choices, the decisions, of individual persons, of organizations of persons, or of social groups. Care must be taken at this stage, however, to ensure that too much is not claimed for the economist. His domain is limited to the behavior of individual persons in choosing among the alternatives open to them. This behavior provides the raw material for the economist, and his theory of economic aggregates is built on foundations of sand if the elemental units, behaving individuals, are overlooked. Individual persons choose among alternatives that they confront; their choices are not mutually exclusive; they do not choose on an either-or basis. Instead, they select the "goods" and reject the "bads" through choices of "more or less." There are few, if any, demonstrably universal goods which are desired independently of quantity variation; and, similarly, there are few, if any, demonstrably universal bads. It is for this reason that the economist does not speak, indeed cannot, of goods and bads separately from the choices made by individual persons.

By examining such choices, the economist can, however, place some restrictions on human behavior patterns. He can develop testable hypotheses about behavior, which observations can refute. Once he has succeeded in identifying what individuals, on the average, regard as "goods," the economist can predict that more of any "good" will be chosen the lower its "price" relative to other goods. This is the central predictive proposition of economics, which can be all-encompassing provided only that the terms *goods* and *price* are defined in sufficiently broad and inclusive ways. This central principle amounts to saying that individuals, when confronted with effective choice, will choose more rather than less.

As such, this remains a very elementary, and, to the economist, self-evident, proposition. But the economist's task is that of extending the range of its application and usefulness. Individuals choose among the various opportunities that they confront, but, in so doing, they cannot treat other individuals as they can the physical environment. One means of choosing more rather than less is choosing to engage in trade; in fact, this is the pervasive means through which man has expanded his command of goods. The institutions of exchange, of markets, are derived, therefore, from the mutual interactions of individuals who are continuously engaged in making ordinary choices for more rather than less. As a "social" scientist, the economist has as his primary function to explain the workings of these institutions and to predict the effects of changes in their structure. As the interaction process that he examines becomes more complex, it is but natural that the task of the economic scientist becomes more intricate. But his central principle remains the same; and he can, through its use, unravel the most tangled sets of structural relationships among human beings.

The economist is able to do this because he possesses this central principle—an underlying theory of human behavior. And because he does so, he qualifies as a scientist and his discipline as a science. What a science does, or should do, is simply to allow the average man, through professional specialization, to command the heights of genius. The basic tools are the simple principles, and these are chained forever to the properly disciplined professional. Without them, he is as a jibbering idiot, who makes only noise under an illusion of speech. The progress of a science is measured by the continuing generalization of its principles, by their extension into new applications. Economics is not different in this respect from any other science. Its progress is best measured by the extent to which its central propositions are pushed outward, are stretched, so to speak, to explain human behavior as yet unexplained, to provide new predictive understanding of institutions emerging from human behavior. Viewed in this light, John von Neumann's contribution lay in extending the principles to apply in a wholly new set of situations confronting the individual. Game theory takes its place within the expanded kit of tools that the economist carries with him.

Contrast this with the Keynesian and post-Keynesian attention on macroeconomics and macroeconomic models. Does this "theory" provide the economist with an additional set of tools? Does this extend the application of the central principles of the discipline? Unfortunately, the answer must be negative here. Precisely because it has divorced itself from the central proposition relating to human behavior, modern macroeconomic theory is really no theory at all. It has evolved, and remains, a set of models for the workings of economic aggregates, models that have little predictive value. Lord Keynes, of course, recognized this, and it was for this reason that he tried to tie his theoretical structure to basic psychological propensities. These propensities, which were designed to replace the more simple neoclassical behavioral propositions, have never fulfilled the role that Keynes must have hoped for them, and the modern model builders seem largely to leave even these out of account.

Macroeconomic theory may, of course, attain the status of science, when and if its propositions carry predictive implications. However, when it does so, it will be a wholly new science, not that of economics. And its practitioners will not be classified by the characteristic responses of economists to the simple conceptual experiment carried out above. It is the divergence of macroeconomics from the central propositions that is tending, today, to create serious problems of communication within the confines of the same discipline that is professionally classified as "economics." Increasingly, it becomes difficult for those who have specialized in macroeconomics to communicate with those who start from the traditional base.

Spillouts to and Spillins from the Neighborhood Sciences—A Schematic Presentation

The discussion to this point has been concerned with what "economics" is. This preliminary has been necessary before raising the main questions of this essay, those which concern the relations of this science to its disciplinary neighbors. Full-length, and useful, methodological essays could, of course, be written covering the relations between economics and each and every one of the neighborhood sciences. Obviously, selectivity and condensation are essential here. It will perhaps be helpful, nonetheless, to present, briefly and schematically, the totality or quasi-totality of relationships. It seems reasonable to think of these as falling broadly within two sets. First, the contributions that economics can make to the other sciences or disciplines can be presented. These external effects can be called "spillouts," following another usage of this term by Burton Weisbrod. Second, the essential contributions that neighborhood disciplines can make to economics may be arrayed. These are, similarly, called "spillins."

In this section I shall present an array of spillouts and spillins, with only limited explanatory discussion under each heading. For simplicity in presentation, I have organized the material so that a single term represents the spillout contribution of economics to each discipline and a single term represents the spillin contribution of each other discipline to economics. Those relationships that will be discussed in more detail in the following section are marked with an asterisk.

What Can Economics Contribute to Its Neighbors?

To Engineering—An Attitude*
To History—Constraints
To Humanities—Dashes of Reality*
To Law—Limitations*
To Mathematics—Applications
To Physical Science—An Appreciation
To Political Science—A Theory*
To Psychology—A Challenge
To Statistics—Problems

The above is, of course, shorthand. And, as with much shorthand, the schema may raise more issues than it resolves. Some brief clarification may be attempted here for those items which cannot be elaborated on in more detail below.

Economics can impose on the study of history essentially a constraining influence. The reconstruction of past events is circumscribed by the predictions that can be made concerning man's responses to his economic environment, and the viability of institutional arrangements may, in a sense, be tested. In fact, one of the interesting developments in economics, which amounts to an extension of its simple principles, involves the work of economic historians in applying data from past years to test the central hypotheses.

Economics offers little to the pure mathematician, at least at firsthand. However, to the applied mathematician, the problems posed by the economist can offer fascinating and fruitful challenges to his ingenuity. And, to the extent that the "twisting" of pure theory by the applied mathematician generates a secondary reaction from the purist, there may be ultimate influence on the development of pure mathematics itself.

The physical scientist can, I think, learn much from the economist. Essentially, he can learn humility as he appreciates the limitations of science and scientific method in application to the inordinately complex problems of human relationships. To the extent that he can learn that, by comparison, his own problems are indeed elementary; despite his great achievements, he becomes both a better scientist and a better citizen.

To the psychologist, the economists offer a standing challenge. Provide us with a better explanatory behavioral hypothesis! Economists know, of course, that ordinary utility maximization does not "explain" all behavior, or even a predominant part of it. Their success is, however, measured by the relevance of this hypothesis. Psychologists object to the economists' behavioral assumptions, but they have not provided sufficiently explanatory alternative hypotheses for the development of a general theory of human behavior in social structure. Perhaps they will do so; the challenge remains with them until they do.

The statistician is in much the same position as the applied mathematician, if, indeed, these two need be distinguished at all. The tests that the economists seek, the aid that they request from him in devising such tests, may open up areas of research that otherwise remain closed.

What Can Economics Learn from Its Neighbors?

From Engineering—A Warning*
From History—Hope
From Humanities—Inspiration
From Law—A Framework*
From Mathematics—A Language
From Physical Science—A Morality*
From Political Science—Data
From Psychology—A Damper
From Statistics—Design*

We may now examine, quite briefly, those spillins to economics, and to economists, from disciplinary neighbors not marked with asterisks on the above listing and thus not reserved for further elaboration.

The idea of progress that pervaded liberal scholarship in the two preceding centuries has, to an extent, disappeared. Nevertheless, history teaches economists, and all others whose subject matter is human civil order, that there is ultimate hope. Man may, and does, behave badly, by almost any standard, on many occasions. Yet learning more about how he does behave can mean only that, ultimately, he may choose to reform his institutions so as to bridle his impulses properly. History should teach the economist that the grievous mistakes of past epochs need not be repeated in the future. History should provide him with hope.

The arts and the humanities have been too long neglected by the economists, through simple error and confusion. The "goods" that men pursue should in no manner of speaking be conceived as vulgarly materialistic, in the commonsense terminology. The economist takes man essentially as he is, and he observes man selecting his own "goods," while shunning his own "bads." But as affluence allows man to rise above the subsistence minima, his "goods" expand to include those things that only the arts and the humanities discuss. Man wants to want better things; he wants to change his own tastes, and he deliberately chooses to modify his own listing of the "goods" that matter to him. It is appropriate that competent research scholars are now devoting attention to the economics of the fine arts.

The language that mathematics provides for economists, supplementary to their own, is widely recognized and understood. Its contribution to the productivity of economists, at the margin, may be questioned, but the integral of the product function must be large indeed.

What can political science, in its traditional disciplinary organization, contribute to the economist? Basically, it provides him with a record, data, of sociopolitical structures that he may, if he chooses, utilize in conducting his conceptual and actual experiments. Governments tend to do many things, and many of them foolishly. Political scientists keep the institutional record.

Psychology always threatens to undermine altogether the economist's simple principles, to make his model as a house of cards. Human behavior is erratic, nonrational, and often wholly unpredictable. Nonlogical explanation often supersedes logical explanation. The psychologist by emphasizing the nonlogical, the "deeper" motivations and urges that guide the human psyche, chips continuously at the economist's predictive models. To an extent, these models remain in a state analogous to Newtonian physics, while the psychologist hopes to achieve the relativity breakthrough. To date, he has not succeeded, but the economist who is wise always keeps out a weather eye.

The two listings, those for spillouts and spillins, are not complete, and the brevity with which the relative directional contributions have been discussed has surely served to confuse as much as to enlighten. And especially for noneconomists, the necessary sketchiness may have served to raise more red flags than intended.

The Important Spillouts from Economics to Neighbor Disciplines

I now propose to discuss the four important spillout relationships marked with asterisks in the above listing more thoroughly.

Engineering

In the simple schema on page 123 I suggested that economics contributes an attitude to the engineer and to the engineering sciences. With the latter term, I refer to all those studies that are instrumentally oriented toward the accomplishment of specific objectives. That is to say, the aim of the science is not understanding, but rather improving, making things work. Under this heading, therefore, I place not only physical engineering, as usually conceived, but also business engineering, most often labeled business administration, and, likewise, social engineering.

As I have suggested, economists have often conceived themselves primarily as social engineers, and their interests have been more oriented to improvements in social structure than to predictions of a scientific character. This has led, and continues to lead, to much confusion. There is, of course, no reason why social engineering need not be a legitimate activity, in certain limits. But the activity of the social engineer is not that of the economic scientist.

Similarly with the business engineer. It is one of the many American tragedies in education that has caused economics to be blanketed with business administration in professional association. Again, the business engineer serves a proper task, but a wholly different one from that of the economist. However, and this should be noted with some emphasis, the business engineer stands in precisely the same relation to the economist as the social engineer. The presumptive arrogance of those who call themselves economists and act as social engineers while scorning the role of the business engineer should be called promptly to account.

Having defined what I mean by "engineering" and "engineer," I can now elaborate what I mean by saying that the economist can contribute an "attitude" that is extremely helpful, as ample evidence reveals. The economist is trained to think in terms of alternatives; his attitude is one of searching among available alternatives for some optimal solution, and the study of the behavior of persons as they carry out such search. Engineers, far too frequently, fail to embody, as a "natural" thought pattern, sufficient concern for *alternatives*. They tend, by contrast, to think in terms of defined objectives and of specific means.

The best examples of the economist's contribution to engineering in this respect is provided by the whole field of operations research. Here the central idea is essentially that of searching out from among the available alternatives and examining the possibility of accomplishing the same objectives with other alternatives, arrayed finally in accordance with some acceptable criteria. A predominant share of the developments in this area of study belongs to those who are trained, professionally, as economists.

The *attitude* that is relevant here is the one which emerges quite naturally from a concentration on the allocation of scarce means among alternative ends—the traditional definition of an economic problem. To many of my professional colleagues, this attitude is the peculiar talent of the economist, and he works always essentially as an engineer. I do not, of course, deny his value to the engineer, be this technical, organizational, or social, but I prefer to divorce this spillout effect from the central principles of economic science. This is not, of course, to deny that the contribution made by economists here is highly productive. It is essential that some professionals specialize, explicitly, in measuring and analyzing the relative costs of alternatives. And, given the state of the scientific world as it is, economists are better equipped to do this than almost anyone else. In the process, however, I should emphasize only that they work as engineers, not as economists.

Humanities

Scholars in the humane studies should maintain at least a nodding acquaintance with economics and with economists. The spillout contribution here is that of imposing reality upon man's natural proclivity to dream. The economist, almost alone, takes man as he exists, and he does not spend his effort in dreaming of man's perfectibility. To the humanist, therefore, the economist's prospect is indeed a dismal one, and his concern with baser motives of man is held to scorn. This is as it should be; the humanist should not be expected to "love" the economist as fellow scholar. Indeed, his very purpose is to stretch the economist's model of ordinary man beyond its natural limits, and his success is measured by his ability to do so. The economist serves to provide the base from which the humanist begins. Essentially, the economist represents an ever-present Hobbesian realism standing counter to the innocent romanticism of all Rousseaus.

Utopianism is not the disease it once was, and to the extent that it has disappeared, the economist's constraints now have less value for the humanist than before. Even the last vestiges of utopianism, represented by the romantic conception of the ever-benevolent bureaucracy, the all-embracing despotism of the state, seem to have been dealt a crushing blow by the turn of events through history. Perhaps there is need now for a new utopianism rather than for its opposite, which seems reflected in the modern waves of disillusionment and despair. What is the future for humane studies in an absurd world? Perhaps the role of the economist has come full circle: Is it too much to claim that sober realism can, in fact, focus renewed attention on attainable human order? When it is finally recognized that man is neither the noble savage nor beset with original sin, the elemental rationality that is central to the economist's model may too become the stuff of dreams.

Law

The medium through which human beings impose constraints on their own interaction, one with another, is provided by the law. The simple principles of economics impose limitations on the operation of these constraints, much as the simple principles of physics impose limitations upon the engineer's working models of machines. Law can modify the conditions under which human beings choose among alternatives; it cannot directly affect the behavior in choosing. Economics seems to generate nonsensical statements by its critics, but none takes precedence over the discussion about the "repeal of the law of supply and demand." Intelligent and sophisticated men, who remain economic illiterates, talk as if human behavior in choice situations could be modified by legal restraints, as opposed to modifications in the conditions for choice. And on the basis of such discussion laws are enacted and enforced which have the effect of preventing the attainment of the very objectives that they are designed to promote.

Minimum-wage laws provide perhaps the best single example. Reasonable men support such legislation on the grounds that the poorer classes will be aided. The effect is, of course, the opposite, as the simplest of economic principles must state. By requiring the payment of a legal minimum wage, employers must choose fewer of the lowest-paid workers rather than more. Low-productivity workers must be unemployed, or must shift into employments not covered by the legal restrictions. The laws harm the poorer and less-productive workers.

Such examples could be multiplied. The laws enacted in the ignorance of simple economic principles can do great damage, yet we observe little progress in the recognition of the limitations that economics should impose on legislation. This is the continuing despair of economists who want to see their science applied in practice.

Political Science

To orthodox political scientists, it may seem the height of presumptive arrogance to say that economics can provide "a theory" for explanation and prediction of political decisions. Nonetheless, it is becoming increasingly evident that the important theoretical advances in the explanation of political phenomena have been made primarily by those who approach the subject matter as economists. The reason for this is not far to seek. The political scientist has not, traditionally, incorporated a theory of human behavior into his structure of political process. To him, theory has never implied prediction. Instead, political theory has suggested normative philosophical discourse on the objectives and aims of political order. Little, if any, positive science is to be found in this tradition.

The economist, shifting his attention to man's behavior in reaching collective decisions in concert with his fellows in some political arrangement, brings with him, ready-made so to speak, a basic behavioral postulate. He is able, through its use, to make predictions, to advance hypotheses that are conceptually refutable. He does so in the full knowledge that the predictive value of his propositions is much less than that of the corresponding propositions relating to man's behavior in the strictly defined market relationship. He is prepared to accept the fact that his "explanation" of politics falls far short of completeness. But he can assert that he has a "theory of politics," of the way men do behave in collective decision-making.

It is essentially this economic approach to politics that has come into attention as an important interdisciplinary area of scholarship since the 1940s. Work here remains in its infancy, but scholarship will surely accelerate over the decades ahead.

Important Spillins to Economics from Other Disciplines

Having discussed the four most important spillouts, the contributions that economics and economists can make to its scientific neighbors, I shall now discuss spillins. The "exchange" among disciplines is clearly multilateral, and the economist can learn much from the larger world of scholarship. Writing this paper as an economist, I find it more difficult to discuss spillins, which are more or less unconsciously allowed to affect our thinking, than I did to discuss spillouts.

Engineering

In the schema above, I have suggested that the contribution of engineering to economics consists of a "warning." Stated in an obverse way, we can say that the engineering sciences offer a constant "temptation" to the economist, and he must ever be on his guard lest he forget his own special position in the scientific world. The argument here is much the same, in reverse, as that offered above concerning the economist's contribution to the engineer. The economist's task is not properly that of *improving,* or making things work, whether these things be technical equipment, a business organization, or the social system. These are engineering tasks, and the economist must warn himself not to assume the role of the engineer too readily. There are specific contributions that the economist can make to engineering, as discussed above. But engineering is engineering, not economics. And the engineer, be he business, social, or technical, can best contribute to the development of economic science if he acts jealously concerning the intrusion of economists into his field. Professionally, the engineer should refuse association with the economist, and he should shun all attempts of the latter to enter into the confines of his discipline. "Management science" should be isolated and should isolate itself from economic science. But so should "social engineering," or "the science of social management," which far too many economists claim as their own bailiwick.

Law

What can the study of law contribute to economics? The answer is clear, but its implications are too often overlooked. Economics seeks to explain human interactions within an emerging-evolving institutional setting, and this setting is best described in terms of the set of laws that conditions human choices. The essential subject matter for the economist consists of human behavior in social institutions, not of human behavior in the abstract. The tendency of economic theorists to overlook this simple fact provoked the reaction of the American institutionalists, a reaction which surely was misguided in its emphasis, but which, nonetheless, pointed up a serious deficiency in the evolution of economic science. Imaginative and critical work in economics remains to be done in extending the applications of principles to the legal setting that is actually observable in a specific society.

To what extent are the rules, the laws, the institutions of social order assumed to be variable in the implied setting of theoretical welfare economics? The economist who has examined this literature will know that there is no answer suggested. Yet it is surely evident that the whole exercise has little significance until such questions are answered. If, in fact, no laws are to be changed, Pareto optimality is automatically attained by each individual acting within the constraints imposed upon him. The whole discussion of Pareto optimality must, therefore, imply some change in the laws governing human conduct. But just which laws are to be subjected to change? Are overriding constitutional provisions to govern the changes that are allowed? These questions shall not be answered here, but merely raising them will suggest the need for some greater tie-in between the structure of economic theory on the one hand and the legal-institutional framework on the other.

How should such work begin? The logical starting place seems to be with the institutional structure that actually is observed. To this factual base can be applied the theoretical analysis. Fruitful results should emerge from such institutional theorizing. It is in such a context that productive work on the economics of property relationships has been done, and is being done, by such economists as Armen Alchian and Ronald Coase.

Physical Science

Frank Knight has said that economists should learn *morals* not method from the physical sciences. There is a point in what Knight says, and it is worth discussing. The physical scientists are scientists in a fuller sense of this emotive term than are most economists. They have been able, with rare exceptions, to conduct reasoned argument critically and dispassionately without the ideological overtones that have plagued effective communication among economists. They have a higher respect for "truth"; at least this appears to be the case to one who stands outside their pavilions. Perhaps this is because their standards are more precise; this, in itself, breeds a scientific morality that social scientists seem to lack. Hobbes is widely credited with having made the statement that general agreement would never have been reached on the proposition that two and two add up to four if it had proved to anyone's interest to argue otherwise. To an extent, this is surely true. The physical sciences have advanced so rapidly because their own advances have been divorced from direct social implications. Economics and economists have been placed at a great disadvantage because they cannot, even if they try, divorce their theory from social implication.

Should economists try to be pure scientists? Should they seek truth independently of values? This continues to be a debated question, and the fact that it is debatable, or thought to be so, suggests the state of the science. Gunnar Myrdal and others argue that there are no independent propositions; that the "truths" in economics emerge from basic value postulates that had best be stated at the outset of discussion. Taken seriously, this position removes all scientific content from the discipline and reduces discussion to a babel of voices making noise. The economist, to maintain his self-respect, must hold fast to the faith that there does exist an independent body of truth in his discipline, truth that can be discerned independently of value judgments.

Theoretical Statistics

Rutledge Vining has impressed upon me the contribution that theoretical statistics can make to the economists and to the study of economics. Practitioners in our discipline have been too prone to look directly at the instantaneously observable results of economic process and to draw from these implications that carry both theoretical and policy content. Statistical theory forces a recognition of the temporal sequences of results that are observable and the variations in distributions over time. The very presence of randomness in the economic universe seems to have been largely neglected in the formal development of the theory that we use. Once we begin to recognize that each and every event in time-space is not predetermined but contains some randomness in its generation, direct inferences from instantaneously observed results become much more difficult.

To what extent can the distribution of income among persons be explained by random variation? To what extent can the distribution of persons over space be explained by random selection? It is clear, once such questions as these are asked, that until we can have some approximate idea as to the answers, we cannot really evaluate the implications of any observable distribution. In designing his conceptual experiments, the economist cannot now fail to allow for the relevance of randomness, or chance, in determining outcomes. This makes the refutation of his hypotheses much more difficult, of course, but it is best that he proceed without false hopes of rigor that does not exist. Truth is not so easy to come by in a world of uncertainty, but, once having recognized this, we are better off as scientists.

Theoretical statistics can contribute to the design of experiments, and to the economist's thinking about design, in yet another way. The statistician recognizes that he does not choose directly among outcomes, allocations, or distributions. His choice is among *rules* that will restrict or confine the range of possible outcomes and among the criteria through which the operation of these rules shall be judged. This attitude is of major importance to the economist, and it can teach him a major lesson. The overemphasis on allocation problems has taught far too many economists to think in terms of directly choosing allocations of resources, distributions of income, etc. Reflection on this indicates at once that such variables are not within the range of social choice, even if social choice be accepted as appropriate for the economist's advice. The society chooses among the several possible rules which restrict or condition human behavior. These rules will generate outcomes, which may be examined in terms of allocations or distributions. Once the emphasis is shifted to the choices among rules, however, the whole structure of discussion of welfare criteria is shifted, and with obvious advantage.

Specialized Interdependence—A Specific Example

Previously I suggested that two trends could be observed in the development of modern economics. First, the independence of the science from its neighbors seems rapidly to be disappearing, while, at the same time, professional specialization within the discipline is proceeding apace. These are, at first glance, contradictory trends, but upon closer examination the contradiction disappears. What seems to be happening in most instances is the emergence of a new orientation of professional specialization, and one that has not, as yet, found its place in the structure of professional organization and educational curricula. It becomes increasingly clear that the channels of effective communication do not extend throughout the discipline that we variously call "economics," and that some "economists" are able to communicate far more effectively with some scholars in the noneconomic disciplines than with those presumably within their own professional category.

I shall illustrate this development, which I think can be generalized for several areas, with reference to a single cross-disciplinary field, one with which I have personally been associated. I refer to the work that has been done by economists in extending the simple principles of their discipline to political decision-making, to the making of decisions in a nonmarket context. As I have suggested earlier, much of the early work was done by economists, but more recently a few political scientists have been directly engaged in this field of scholarship. At the same time separate but closely related work has been done in other areas. Economists who have worked on the "theory of teams," on the "economics of information," on the "theory of organization" have all been concerned with similar constructions. Psychologists who have been concerned with small-group theory, all scholars who have worked in game theory, and especially with nonzero sum cooperative games, also fall into the cross-disciplinary field that is emerging. There are even a few philosophers who, in their concern with what is called "rule-utilitarianism," fall into the interdisciplinary communication network.

Through this development, it becomes far easier, and more interesting as well as more productive, for the economist who works with nonmarket decisions to communicate with the positive political scientist, the game theorist, or the organizational theory psychologist than it is for him to communicate with the growth-model macroeconomist, with whom he scarcely finds any common ground. This specialized interdependence, if it is, in fact, general over several emerging specializations, can be expected to result, ultimately, in some movements toward professional institutionalization. To an extent, this has already happened in such areas as regional science. These movements should not be discouraged by the inherent conservatism of established disciplinary orthodoxy. Insofar as interdisciplinary specialization emerges genuinely from the changing channels of effective scholarly communication, steps taken to further such communication, while breaking down traditionally established disciplinary lines, represent added efficiency.

Conclusions

The starting point for this essay has been the empirical embodiment of economics as a scientific discipline. I have deliberately interpreted economics narrowly, as a science and as a positive set of conceptually refutable propositions about human behavior in a social organization. The normative content that is often alleged to be present in the discipline has been simply defined as outside the pale of discussion here. This is, I think, as it should be, although I recognize that many highly competent methodologists will sharply disagree with my position on this. There is, I submit, positive content to the science that is economics, and it is this positive content that is currently deserving of stress and emphasis, both on the part of its own practitioners and on that of its neighboring scholars. The role of the economist, at base, must be that of attempting to understand a certain type of human behavior and the prediction of the social structures that are emergent from that behavior. Ultimately, the economist must hope that his simple truths, as extended, can lead to "improvement" in the structure of these institutions, through the ability of institutions to modify the conditions of human choice. But improvement must remain his secondary and subsidiary purpose; he verges dangerously on irresponsible action when he allows his zeal for social progress, as he conceives this, to take precedence over his search for and respect of scientific truth, as determined by the consensus of his peers.

This does not imply that the economic scientist must remain in the realm of pure theory and shun all discussions of economic policy. There can be, and should be, a theory of economic policy. And the economist, by analyzing the results of alternative lines of action, can be of great assistance to the social decision-maker. But, as such, the economist has no business at playing the social engineer. He can hope that his light will ultimately be used to generate some heat, but he should live with his hope and refuse to become an activist. He can point out to men the opportunities for reorganizing their social institutions in such a way as to achieve the goals that men desire. But the final choices in a free society rest with individuals who participate in that society. Men may choose to live primitively and to refuse to recognize the simple principles that economists continually repeat. If they so choose, they will so choose, and it is not the task of the economist, or anyone else, to say that they "should" necessarily choose differently. The task of the economist, and of economic science, is done when the simple propositions are presented.

If the economist can learn from his colleagues in the physical sciences, and learn in sufficient time, that the respect for truth takes precedence above all else and that it is the final value judgment that must pervade all science, he may, yet, rescue the discipline from its currently threatened rush into absurdity, oblivion, and disrepute. In the large, he does not seem to be learning, and, if anything, the physical scientist seems more in danger of accepting the perverted confusion that has plagued the economist through generations. But there are a few encouraging signs, and these are to be found in the genuinely exciting areas of specialized interdisciplinary interdependence that are in full flower. A second ray of hope lies in the attitude of the young scholars, in economics as well as its neighbors. Their attitude is properly critical of all ideologues. To the emotionally committed socialist or libertarian, who parades also as economist, these young scholars may appear as disinterested, lacking passion, as "cold fish." But to the extent that they are, economics is gaining stature as a science and is shedding its burdensome overgrowth of social involvement. The economics that may gain full stature as a science will not excite the reformers who have occupied too many of its chairs in past decades, but to those who seek for truth the discipline will be worthy of their efforts.

The challenge remains with those who are and will become economists. The pessimist observes the prostitution and worries about scientific morality. The optimist seizes the rays of hope and projects the millennium. The final response will depend perhaps as much upon the unpredictable evolution of social institutions, guided only in part by rational choices, as on the deliberate decisions made by the professionals.

7

An Economist's Approach to "Scientific Politics"

It is sometimes useful to force scholars outside of political science who look upon government and politics to tell what they may see. This aim is suggestive of the fable about the blind men and the elephant. The point that I should like to draw from this fable is not, however, the familiar one. It should be obvious that a group of reasonable blind men would compare notes one with another, and upon so doing, they should, collectively, be able to put together a fair picture of the elephant after all. In matters of scientific import, we are all blind, although some of us may be blinder than others. And one way of living with our inherent blindness is that of getting together and comparing notes with others who we know have approached the common subject matter from different vantage points, through different windows, to use Nietzsche's appropriate metaphor. Of course, my inference here is valid only if we are somehow assured that we are all examining the same elephant, and when we substitute *government* and *politics* for the

This chapter is reprinted without substantial change from *Perspectives in the Study of Politics*, ed. M. Parsons (Chicago: Rand-McNally, 1968), pp. 77–88. Permission to reprint is herewith acknowledged.

word *elephant,* I am not at all certain that we are. There would be little point in the blind men comparing notes if some of them should be describing their contacts with an elephant and others with an ostrich.

As a very first step, therefore, let me define what it is that I shall be talking about when I use the words *government* and *politics,* and when I try to discuss the approach to these that is taken, or may be taken, by the economist. Actually, as you will see, I shall discuss the approach that I think should be taken by the economist. Most scholars who now call themselves economists take an approach different from my own, and one that I regard as both confused and wrong. In my vision of social order, individual persons are the basic component units, and "government" is simply that complex of institutions through which individuals make collective decisions, and through which they carry out collective as opposed to private activities. "Politics" is the activity of persons in the context of such institutions. These definitions perhaps seem simple ones, and you may find them broadly acceptable. Nevertheless, there are implications of these definitions which may not be so evident at the outset. In my vision, or my model, individual persons are the ultimate decision-makers, and if we want to discuss governmental decision processes we must analyze the behavior of individuals as they participate in these processes. We do not conceive government as some supraindividual decision-making agency, one that is separate and apart from the individual persons for whom choices are being made. In other terms, I stress the "by the people" leg of the Lincoln triad. Most modern analysts, including most economists, place almost exclusive emphasis on the "for the people" leg. Government is, presumably, for the people, but people are rarely allowed to count in determining what is for them. Most economists and, I suspect, most political scientists, view government as a potentially benevolent despot, making decisions in the "general" or the "public" interest, and they deem it their own social function to advise and counsel this despot on, first, the definition of this general interest and, second, the means of furthering it. They rarely will admit all this quite so bluntly as I have put it here, but surely this is the honest way of stating the prevailing methodological orthodoxy. This position is, of course, a relatively happy one for the political economist. Once he has defined his social welfare function, his public interest, he can advance solutions to all of society's economic ills, solutions that government, as *deus ex machina,* is, of course, expected to implement. Politics, the behavior of ordinary men in this process, becomes tainted activity, albeit necessary in a begrudgingly admitted way. But politics should be allowed to interfere as little as is possible with the proper business of government. So runs the orthodoxy. You can add the illustrative refrains better than I can to this beginning verse.

The role of the social scientist who adopts broadly democratic models of the governmental process, who tries to explain and to understand how people do, in fact, govern *themselves,* is a less attractive one than the role that is assumed by the implicit paternalist. The social function is not that of improving anything directly; instead, it is that of explaining behavior of a certain sort which, only remotely and indirectly, can lead to improvements in the political process itself.

Now let me return to the initial question. If we should agree that what we are looking at is the complex set of institutional interactions among individual persons which is generated as a result of their attempts to accomplish mutually desired goals collectively, if this is what we mean by government, then my problem becomes: How does the economist view this set of institutions, and how does his own professional competence and prejudice affect his "vision"? And of what value can his interpretations of behavior be to the political scientist?

This leads me once again to basic methodological definitions. What is economics all about? And here, as I suggested, I find myself a heretic, for I think that most economists do not know. I think that they are hopelessly bogged down in methodological confusion, a confusion that threatens to destroy the whole discipline. Economics is about the economy. We can all agree on this. But what is the economy? We are back where we were with government. I define the economy in precisely the same way that I defined government. It is that complex of institutions that emerges as a result of the behavior of individual persons who organize themselves to satisfy their various objectives privately, as opposed to collectively. Thus, the economy and the government are parallel sets of institutions, similar in many respects, and, of course, intersecting at many separate points. In neither case is it appropriate for the analyst, the scientist if you will, to do more than explain the working of these institutions. It is wholly beyond his task for the economist to define goals or objectives of the economy or of the government and then to propose measures designed to implement these goals. The economist who claims professional sanction to say that protective tariffs are bad is on all fours with the political scientist who claims sanction to say that the Congress is an inefficient decision-maker. Both are wholly outside their appropriate professional roles. This kind of confusion dominates both disciplinary fields.

The economist, then, observes people as they behave in the institutional structure that, for convenience, we refer to as the economy, and he then attempts to explain this behavior. It would be fair to ask at this point whether or not I am proposing a return to the institutional economics that was propounded by a group of scholars in the United States in the 1920s, notably by Veblen, Mitchell, and Commons. My answer is an ambivalent one. The institutionalists were broadly on target in many of their criticisms of orthodoxy; but their whole effort was largely wasted because of their scorn of theory, of analysis. Their methodological naiveté caused them to think that observation and description somehow automatically give rise to predictive theories, to hypotheses, when, in fact, we now know that almost the reverse holds. What I am calling for, as the proper function of economists, is institutional theory or institutional analysis, which involves in many cases the use of highly rarefied and abstract models, the implications of which can be checked by real-world observations. Much of modern economic theory can be made to fit the disciplinary pattern that I am outlining. We first try to create a logically consistent theory of individual behavior in the marketplace and then we try, as best we can, to test the implications of this theory against real-world observations. In this way, after much trial and error, we make, I hope, some scientific progress.

My professional and methodological prejudices suggest that the study of government should be approached in the same way. We should try to derive a theory of individual behavior in the political process, and then we should try to check out the implications of the theory against the facts. When I looked around at all this, some dozen years ago, I was surprised to find that a theory of individual behavior in political process did not exist, and that only a few scattered attempts had ever been made to create one. This demonstrated, to me, that there was at least this one rather profound difference between the development of economic and political "science," and it also suggested that there was, perhaps, a function for the economist who was willing to shift his emphasis from market processes to political processes. Since that time, since 1954 roughly speaking, I have been, in the on-and-off manner of academic custom, working within this broadly defined area of research. That is to say, I have been exploring, along with various colleagues and coworkers, some of the aspects of a theory of individual behavior in political choice.

My focus has been dramatically different from that of the orthodox political scientist who looks first at government as the entity, and then discusses its formation, evolution, and operation. To develop any theory of individual behavior, by contrast with this, we must look first at the individual person, at his private behavior as he participates in collective decision-making with his fellows. If we are to move beyond description here, however, if we are to derive any theory worthy of serious consideration, we find it essential to invent simple models of the whole political process. Only in this manner does it become possible to select, to reduce the complexity to manageable, discussable proportions, to abstract from the inessential elements while concentrating on the essential ones. Accepting the overall vision of government that I have mentioned above, the appropriate model within which to begin to examine individual behavior seemed to be that of pure democracy, in the town-meeting sense. In my first paper on this subject, therefore, I tried to contrast the behavior of the single individual in the market-place and in voting under pure democracy.

I should mention that I was directly stimulated to think about all this, an economist thinking about politics, not by some independent discovery on my own part, but by an intuitive dissatisfaction with the book by Kenneth Arrow, published in 1951, and entitled *Social Choice and Individual Values*.[1] In this justly praised little book, Arrow employed the tools of modern symbolic logic and mathematics to show that the construction of a consistent and reasonably acceptable social welfare function from a set of unchanging individual preference orderings was logically impossible if the political decision rule should be that of simple majority voting. That is to say, Arrow demonstrated that majority voting could not be depended upon to produce a consistent set of social decisions. The paradox of voting was not, of course, new with Arrow; it had been known for decades by a small group of specialists who had concerned themselves about the theory of voting, notably Lewis Carroll, and it had been discussed more recently by Duncan Black, about whom more will be said later in this paper. But Arrow was the first to place the paradox of voting in a broader context, in his case that of theoretical welfare economics, and his work did serve to draw the attention of scholars, both in economics and in politics, to the paradox.

---

[1] Kenneth Arrow, *Social Choice and Individual Values* (New York: John Wiley & Sons, 1951).

As I said, I was unhappy with the Arrow book, and more importantly, with all of its reviewers, for a failure to sense what was, to me, a very significant aspect of constitutional democracy. Arrow, and all of his reviewers, seemed unhappy with his general conclusion; they seemed to feel that things would have been so much nicer had his proof turned out the other way. It would have made for a more satisfactory social science if only majority voting could have been shown to produce a set of wholly consistent choices. Consistency in *social* choice seemed to be the criterion that was overriding in the general commentary. This suggested to me that neither Arrow nor his critics were talking about the same elephant that I thought about when I conceived government or politics, or majority rule. It appeared to me, and still does, that decisions made by voting majorities are acceptable, tolerably so, only to the extent that these majorities are shifting and unstable. If we had a majority voting rule that would, in fact, produce internally consistent choices in the Arrow sense, we should, indeed, have a tyranny of the majority. From all this, I concluded[2] that despite the fact that his whole structure of analysis was based on individual preference orderings, Arrow did not conceive governmental process as emerging basically from individual values.

In any case, I began to look somewhat further into the developments in theoretical welfare economics from the vantage point of a specialist in tax and expenditure decisions. Modern welfare economics owes its stimulus to Pareto, who developed a criterion, admittedly a very re-

---

[2] James M. Buchanan, "Social Choice, Democracy, and Free Markets," *Journal of Political Economy* 62 (April 1954): 114–23.

stricted one which enables social situations or positions to be classified into nonoptimal and optimal sets without requiring that interpersonal comparisons of utility be made, or external ethical norms be introduced. Pareto's criterion is simply that which defines a position as optimal if no changes from that position can be made without making at least one person in the group worse off. Admittedly, there are an infinite number of such positions, but the criterion does at least allow for the classification of all possible positions into the two categories. It does not, of course, provide any assistance at all in selecting from among all the optimal positions that which is somehow globally best. Economists who wanted to say a lot about public policy issues were not at all happy with the Pareto criterion. Therefore, they reintroduced interpersonal comparability in the form of an externally defined social welfare function, which they admitted to be dependent on explicit ethical norms. But, of course, there are as many social welfare functions as there are people to define them; in this sense, the notion is equivalent in all respects with the political scientists' conception of the public interest.

My own inclination was, and is, to throw out the whole social welfare function apparatus, which only confuses the issues, and to see what the full implications of the Pareto criterion might be. If we are willing to use the Pareto criterion where it is applicable and simply to admit our inability, as scientists, to say anything where the criterion cannot be applied, some worthwhile content remains in welfare economics. But this raises another question of fundamentals. How are we, as external observers, to know when a person is, in fact, better off or worse off? Here there admits of only one answer. We can judge the better-offness and worse-offness only by observing individual choices. If a man is observed to choose situation A when he could have remained in situation B, we say that he is better off in A, as revealed to us by his own actions. This is not, of course, to say that individuals do not make mistakes or that they always know with certainty which of a set of alternative outcomes will make them better off *ex post facto*. The implication here is only that the individual, observed to make his own choices, is a better judge of his own better-offness than is any external observer of his behavior. This implication amounts to an explicit value judgment, admittedly so, but it is the value judgment upon which Western liberal society has been founded.

Starting with nothing more than this, how far can we go in analyzing political behavior? Two separate lines of advance seem to be suggested. First of all, commencing with a set of individual preferences along with a given rule for reaching group decisions, we may examine and analyze the results. That is, essentially, the route taken in the pioneer works of Duncan Black, whose theory of committees and election[3] continues to be unduly neglected, both by political scientists and by economists. As Black suggests, this is pure theorizing about politics, and, as such, it is wholly devoid of normative content. Black is concerned exclusively with the prediction of the outcomes of certain rules for the making of group choices, specifically with majority rule, given a set of individual preference patterns.

Almost always, however, pure analysis has some normative implications, if not immediate normative content, and

---

[3] Duncan Black, *Theory of Committees and Elections* (Cambridge: At the University Press, 1958).

even Black in his purely theoretical works was motivated to search for alternatives to simple majority voting in order to surmount the obstacles posed by the paradox, by the cyclical majority, by the probability that no majority motion would be located. His work on the various schemes of Lewis Carroll, Borda, Condorcet, stands unique in the literature. Lying close to the surface of Black's work has been his implicit value position to the effect that, if it could be located and if it did exist, the majority motion or the majority solution *should* be the one adopted. Note that the underlying judgment is, in many respects, similar to that which can be criticized in relation to Arrow's work.

My own thinking has proceeded along a second, and alternative, path. In my own set of value judgments, there is nothing even remotely sacrosanct about the will of a simple majority of voters in an election. Influenced strongly by the thinking of Knut Wicksell,[4] a famous, if eccentric, Swedish economist, and coming to an analysis of politics out of a background of public finance, the rule of unanimity seemed to me to possess qualities that have largely been ignored. This, rather than majority rule, seemed to be the base, the reference point from which further discussion and theorizing about political choice must begin. If we reject the notion that there must exist a public or general interest apart from that of the participants, we are necessarily led to the conclusion that only upon unanimous consent of all parties can we be absolutely assured that the total welfare of the group is improved. As applied to politics, the rule of unanimity is equivalent to the Pareto cri-

---

[4] Knut Wicksell, *Finanztheoretische Untersuchungen* (Jena: Gustav Fisher, 1896).

terion for judging a potential change to be optimal. Not only does majority voting lead to paradoxes, to cycles, but also, majority voting, under familiar institutional conditions, leads to a wastage of economic resources, as Gordon Tullock first demonstrated.[5]

At this point, the direction of analysis of political institutions seemed to be that of trying to reconcile, if at all possible, the widely observed use of majority and plurality devices for reaching group choices with the demonstrably inefficient results, in a resource allocative sense, that these devices surely produce. This led Tullock and me to ask the simple question: Why should an individual, if he were given the opportunity, ever choose to be governed by the majority voting of his fellows? Once we had posed the question, and almost before we knew it ourselves, we found ourselves in an economic theory of the political constitution. If one begins to approach the study of political institutions in this way—that is, from the reference position of the single individual in the group—one begins soon to see that a "logical" explanation of the political constitution can be derived. In a very preliminary way, such an explanation was advanced in our book, *The Calculus of Consent,* published in 1962.[6]

What I have done is to outline, in a shorthand sense, the way that one economist has looked, and looks, at government. Now let me turn to the second part of my task. I have talked almost exclusively about how an economist's approach to government, to political process, can be helpful,

---

[5] Gordon Tullock, "Some Problems of Majority Voting," *Journal of Political Economy* 67 (December 1959): 571–79.

[6] James M. Buchanan and Gordon Tullock, *The Calculus of Consent* (Ann Arbor: University of Michigan Press, 1962).

how this may be able to lead to fruitful explanation. I have not yet talked about how the extension and application of the economist's frame of reference can be helpful in analyzing politics in its most general sense. Politics is concerned with the behavior of politicians, not with the behavior of individual voters, and in real-world institutions, persons vote for or against politicians normally, not for or against proposals, as is assumed in the simple town-meeting models implicit in the general theory of committees and of constitutions. Also, politicians, in some more general sense of the word, inhabit the bureaucracy, and their behavior in this role also requires analysis. How can the approach of the economist be of assistance in analyzing the behavior of politicians?

Again, the more or less natural proclivity of economists is to look at individual behavior, at individual choice, and this has led, and is leading, to useful results. Anthony Downs, in his book *An Economic Theory of Democracy,*[7] analyzes the operation of a party system of government in terms of the attempts of party politicians to maximize votes, analogous to the behavior of businessmen in attempting to maximize profits. Somewhat more generally, Gordon Tullock applied the approach that may be called methodological individualism to the whole structure of political relationships, including specifically bureaucratic hierarchies. He commenced the analysis of bureaucracy by looking directly at the set of rewards and punishments that confront the bureaucrat, as he finds himself situated in the hierarchy. This seems a simple starting point, but it is one that tradi-

---

[7] Anthony Downs, *An Economic Theory of Democracy* (New York: Harper & Bros., 1957).

tional scholars in administration have rarely taken and it is one that, when once taken, opens up whole areas of interesting research and analysis, including hypotheses that can be empirically tested. Tullock's formidable work on this subject, *The Politics of Bureaucracy,*[8] although just formally published in 1965, through its preliminary version, privately circulated in 1959, had already made its impact on thinking about bureaucracy. In this treatment of the "politics of the lower order," he compares the different worlds of bureaucrats and professional politicians. He analyzes their role perceptions and their interactions. The impact came, however, not through any influence on the thinking of those who have worked within the traditional methodology of administration but, instead, through its influence on those few economists who, being generally responsive to the Tullockian approach, have been willing to shift their attention to bureaucracy as an object of analysis.

Thus it is that Anthony Downs, an economist now with the RAND Corporation, has been recently engaged in what is possibly the most interesting research on bureaucracy that is under way anywhere. His *Inside Bureaucracy* proceeds from the assumption that all bureaucrats, to some extent, act in their own self-interest. From this and related assumptions Downs develops a theory of organizational behavior which encompasses a range of activities including bureau life cycles, types of bureaucrats, problems of communication, goal consensus, and the relationship between individual freedom and the increasing bureaucratization of

---

[8] Gordon Tullock, *The Politics of Bureaucracy* (Washington: Public Affairs Press, 1965).

modern society.[9] He has worked closely at RAND with Roland McKean, who, having applied an approach similar to Tullock's (which he developed independently) to town planning in Great Britain, is now analyzing the structure of the national defense establishment in the United States.[10]

This whole area of investigation, that is, that which is devoted to an analysis of the behavior of the politician in bureaucracy, is now only on the threshold of its development. It is an exciting field. It is one which allows the analyst to bring theoretical models into contact with institutional reality, to test his hypotheses against observable facts.

You may be prompted to ask: Why do I claim so much here? How does the economist's approach to politics and government differ from that which the habitual political scientist adopts? As I have tried to indicate, the shift in thinking is a simple one. It involves only the shift from the organizational entity as the unit to the individual-in-the-organization. Instead of trying to examine the institutions of politics as organizations, the whole approach involves trying to examine the interactions among individuals as they carry out assigned roles within these institutions.

I am probably more vulnerable if you should object that I claim too much for the economist, as such, in developing the approach to government and politics that I have broadly outlined. Certainly, as economics is currently conceived by most scholars who call themselves economists, there is no

---

[9] Anthony Downs, *Inside Bureaucracy, How Large Organizations Behave* (Boston: Little, Brown, 1967).

[10] Roland N. McKean, "Divergencies Between Individual and Total Costs Within Government," *American Economic Review* (May 1964).

particular contribution of the sort mentioned that emerges necessarily out of their concentration on governmental processes. The great majority of modern economists do not really think much about the process of government, and when they do, they adopt implicitly the same broad conceptions that the orthodox political scientist adopts explicitly. Hence, when I submit to you that there has been exciting work done recently on government and politics, and that this work has been mostly done by economists, I am really talking about a small group of mavericks, a few oddballs, a few eccentrics, who have not yet commanded much attention, even among economists, and certainly not among many political scientists. But the ranks of this small group are gradually swelling, the list of books grows longer year by year, and recognition is being granted. I speak, of course, out of personal prejudice here, but I think that an exciting and new field of theoretical inquiry is emerging on the borderline between two disciplines. This new field does not as yet have an appropriate descriptive name, and certainly the rubric "scientific politics" that I have rather boldly used in the title to this paper is not wholly suitable. Professional political scientists are beginning to work in this area along with the few economists, and the concentration promises to attract more and more young scholars in the decade just ahead.[11]

The approach is scientific in a genuine meaning of this term, something which the approach of traditional political

---

[11] William C. Mitchell, "The Shape of Political Theory to Come: From Political Sociology to Political Economy" (mimeographed, 1967), a paper delivered at the 63d Annual Meeting of the American Political Science Association, September 1967, that is extremely encouraging in these respects.

science can scarcely claim. If, in fact, a pure theory of politics or a genuinely scientific politics is to be developed, the individualistic model that I have discussed here will be an important element in its source. To make this claim does, I appreciate, make traditionalists rise up in anger, and it is admittedly presumptuous on my part to advance it. Indeed, as a recent friendly critic put it, my tone here may seem messianic, and I suppose that it is. I am, personally, both involved in and excited about the contribution that the new scientific politics can make to our overall understanding of both government and politics. And I find it personally satisfying to participate directly in what is surely an emerging area of research and scholarly emphasis.

In partial apology, however, I should stress that I claim for my approach to the new scientific politics no exclusive domain. While I am convinced that it can be helpful in explaining real-world political phenomena, I know that many other models of analysis, such as statistical decision theory, game theory communications theory, and others, can also be fruitful. Hence, I say only that here is an additional and supplementary set of tools which I hope more and more students of government and politics will learn to use. To return once again to the fable of the blind men and the elephant, the supplementary set of tools that this approach to scientific politics offers is just one more blind man added to the circle; that is all. But, by adding its own contribution to the collective discourse, to the collective wisdom of the existing world of scholarship, which, in effect, involves only a continuing comparing of notes, a somewhat better, although still imperfect, picture of the elephant may be drawn.

8

Foreword to Tullock's
The Politics of Bureaucracy

I t is not from the benevolence of the butcher, the brewer, or the baker, that we expect our dinner, but from their regard to their own interest." This statement is, perhaps, the most renowned in the classic book in political economy, Adam Smith's *Wealth of Nations*. From Smith onward, the appropriate function of political economy, and political economists, has been that of demonstrating how the market system, as a perfectible social organization, can, and to an extent does, channel the private interests of individuals toward the satisfaction of desires other than their own. Insofar as this cruder instinct of man toward acquisitiveness, toward self-preservation, can be harnessed through the interactions of the market mechanism, the necessity for reliance on the nobler virtues, those of benevolence and self-sacrifice, is minimized. This fact, as Sir Dennis Robertson has so eloquently reminded us, gives the economist a reason for existing, and his "warning bark" must be heeded by those decision-makers who fail to recognize the need for economizing on "love."

This chapter is reprinted from Gordon Tullock, *The Politics of Bureaucracy* (Washington: Public Affairs Press, 1965), pp. 1–9. Permission to reprint is herewith acknowledged.

Despite such warning barks (and some of these have sounded strangely like shouts of praise), the politicians for many reasons have, over the past century, placed more and more burden of organized social activity on political, governmental processes. As governments have been called upon to do more and more important things, the degree of popular democratic control over separate public or governmental decisions has been gradually reduced. In a real sense, Western societies have attained universal suffrage only after popular democracy has disappeared. The electorate, the ultimate sovereign, must, to an extent not dreamed of by democracy's philosophers, be content to choose its leaders. The ordinary decisions of government emerge from a bureaucracy of ever-increasing dimensions. Nongovernmental and quasi-governmental bureaucracies have accompanied the governmental in its growth. The administrative hierarchy of a modern corporate giant differs less from the federal bureaucracy than from the freely contracting tradesmen envisaged by Adam Smith.

This set, this drift, of history toward bigness, in both "public" and in "private" government, has caused many a cowardly scholar to despair and to seek escape by migrating to a dream world that never was. It has caused other "downstream" scholars to snicker with glee at the apparent demise of man, the individual. In this book, by contrast, Tullock firmly grasps the nettle offered by the modern bureaucratic state. In effect, he says: "If we must have bureaucratic bigness, let us, at the least, open our eyes to its inner workings. Man does not simply cease to exist because he is submerged in an administrative hierarchy. He remains an individual, with individual motives, impulses, and desires." This seems a plausible view of things. But, and surprisingly, we find that few theorists of bureaucracy have started from this base. Much of administrative theory, ancient or modern, is based on the contrary view that man becomes as a machine when he is placed within a hierarchy, a machine that faithfully carries out the orders of its superiors who act for the whole organization in reaching policy decisions. Tullock returns us to Adam Smith's statement, and he rephrases it as follows: "It is not from the benevolence of the bureaucrat that we expect our research grant or our welfare check, but out of his regard to his own, not the public interest."

Adam Smith and the economists have been, and Tullock will be, accused of discussing a world peopled with evil and immoral men. Men "should not" be either "getting and spending" or "politicking." Such accusations, and they never cease, are almost wholly irrelevant. Some social critics simply do not like the world as it is, and they refuse to allow the social scientist, who may not like it either, to analyze reality. To the scientist, of course, analysis must precede prescription, and prescription must precede improvement. The road to utopia must start from here, and this road cannot be traversed until here is located, regardless of the beautiful descriptions of yonder. Tullock's analysis is an attempt to locate the "here" in the real, existing, world of modern bureaucracy. His assumptions about behavior in this world are empirical, not ethical. He is quite willing to leave the test of his model to the reader and to future scholars. If, in fact, men in modern bureaucracy do not seek "more" rather than "less," measured by their own career advancement, when they are confronted with relevant choices, Tullock would readily admit the failure of his model to be explanatory in other than some purely tautological sense.

When it is admitted, as all honesty suggests, that some individuals remain individuals, even in a bureaucratic hierarchy, Tullock's analysis assumes meaning. It provides the basis for discussing seriously the prospects for improving the "efficiency" of these bureaucratic structures in accomplishing the tasks assigned to them. There are two stages in any assessment of the efficiency of organizational hierarchies, just as there are in the discussions of the efficiency of the market organization. First, there must be a description, an explanation, a theory, of the behavior of the individual units that make up the structure. This theory, as in the theory of markets, can serve two purposes and, because of this, methodological confusion is compounded. Such an explanatory, descriptive, theory of individual behavior can serve a normative purpose, can provide a guide to the behavior of an individual unit which accepts the objectives or goals postulated in the analytical model. In a wholly different sense, however, the theory can serve a descriptive, explanatory function in a positive manner, describing the behavior of the average or representative unit, without normative implications *for* behavior of any sort. This important distinction requires major stress here. It has never been fully clarified in economic theory, where the contrast is significantly sharper than in the nascent political theory that Tullock and a few others are currently attempting to develop.

The analogy with the theory of the firm is worth discussing in some detail here. This theory of the firm, an individual unit in the organized market economy, serves two purposes. It may, if properly employed, serve as a guide to a firm that seeks to further the objectives specified in the model. As such, the theory of the firm falls wholly outside economics, political economy, and, rather, falls within business administration or managerial science. Essentially the same analysis may, however, be employed, by the economist, as a descriptive theory that helps the student of market organization to understand the workings of this system which is necessarily composed of individual units.

Tullock's theory of the behavior of the individual "politician" in bureaucracy can be, and should be, similarly interpreted. Insofar as such units, the "politicians," accept the objectives postulated—in this case, advancement in this administrative hierarchy—Tullock's analysis can serve as a "guide" to the ambitious bureaucrat. To think primarily of the analysis in this light would, in my view, be grossly misleading. Instead the analysis of the behavior of the individual politician should be treated as descriptive and explanatory, and its validity should be sought in its ability to assist us in the understanding of the operation of bureaucratic systems generally.

Once this basic theory of the behavior of the individual unit is constructed, it becomes possible to begin the construction of a theory of the inclusive system, which is composed of a pattern of interactions among the individual units. By the nature of the systems with which he works, administrative hierarchies, Tullock's "theory of organization" here is less fully developed than is the analogous "theory of markets." A more sophisticated theory may be possible here, and, if so, Tullock's analysis can be an important helpmate to whoever chooses to elaborate it.

Finally, the important step can be taken from positive analysis to normative prescription, not for the improvement of the strategically oriented behavior of the individual unit directly, but for the improvement in the set of working rules that describe the organization. This step, which must be the ultimate objective of all social science, can only be taken after the underlying theory has enabled the observer to make some comparisons among alternatives. The last half of this book is primarily devoted to the development of such norms for "improving" the functioning of organizational hierarchies.

Tullock's "politician" is, to be sure, an "economic" man of sorts. No claim is made, however, that this man, this politician, is wholly descriptive of the real world. More modestly, Tullock suggests (or should do so, if he does not) that the reference politician is an ideal type, one that we must recognize as being always a part of reality, although he does not, presumably, occupy existing bureaucratic structures to the exclusion of all other men. One of Tullock's primary contributions, or so it appears to me, lies in his ability to put flesh and blood on the bureaucratic man, to equip him with his own power to make decisions, to take action. Heretofore, theorists of bureaucracy, to my knowledge, have not really succeeded in peopling their hierarchies. What serves to motivate the bureaucrat in modern administrative theory? I suspect that one must search at some length to find an answer that is as explicit as that provided by Tullock. Because explicit motivation is introduced, a model containing predictive value can be built, and the predictions can be conceptually refuted by appeal to evidence. It is difficult to imagine how a "theory" of bureaucracy in any meaningful sense could be begun in any other way.

By implication, my comments to this point may be interpreted to mean that Tullock's approach to a theory of administration is an "economic" one, and that the most accurate shorthand description of this book would be to say that it represents an "economist's" approach to bureaucracy. This would be, in one sense, correct, but at the same time such a description would tend to cloud over and to subordinate Tullock's second major contribution. This lies in his sharp dichotomization of the "economic" and the "political" relationships among men. Since this book is devoted almost exclusively to an examination of the political relationship, it has little that is economic in its content. It represents an economist's approach to the political relationship among individuals. This is a more adequate summary, but this, too, would not convey to the prospective reader who is unfamiliar with Tullock's usage of the particular words the proper scope of the analysis. I have, in the discussion above, tried to clarify the meaning of the economist's approach. There remains the important distinction between the economic and the political relationship.

This distinction is, in one sense, the central theme of the book. In a foreword, it is not proper to quarrel with an author's usage, but synonyms are sometimes helpful in clearing away ambiguities. Tullock distinguishes, basically, between the relationship of *exchange,* which he calls the economic, and the relationship of *slavery,* which he calls the political. I emphasize these words here, and do so deliberately. In its pure or ideal form, the superior-inferior relationship is that of the master and the slave. If the inferior has no alternative means of improving his own well-being other than through pleasing his superior, he is, in fact, a "slave," pure and simple. This remains true quite independently of the particular institutional constraints that may or may not inhibit the behavior of the superior. It matters not whether the superior can capitalize the human personality of the inferior and market him as an asset. Interestingly enough, the common usage of the word *slavery* refers to an institutional structure in which exchange was a dominant relationship. In other words, to the social scientist at any rate, the mention of slavery calls to mind the exchange process, with the things exchanged being slaves. The word itself does not particularize the relationship between master and slave at all. Thus, as with so many instances in Tullock's book, we find no words that describe adequately the relationships that he discusses. Examples, however, serve to clarify. Would I be less a slave if you as my master could not exchange me, provided only that I have no alternative source of income? My income may depend exclusively on my pleasing you, my master, despite the fact that you too may be locked into the relationship. Serfdom, as distinct from slavery, may be a more descriptive term, especially since Tullock finds many practical examples for his analysis in feudal systems.

The difficulty in explaining the political relationship in itself attests to the importance of Tullock's analysis, and, as he suggests, the whole book can be considered a definition of this relationship. The sources of the difficulty are apparent. First of all, the political relationship is not commonly encountered in its pure form, that of abject slavery as noted above. By contrast, its counterpart, the economic or exchange relationship, is, at least conceptually, visualized in its pure form and, in certain instances, the relationship actually exists. This amounts to saying that, without quite realizing what we are doing, we think of ourselves as free men living in a free society. The economic relationship comes more or less naturally to us as the appropriate organizational arrangement through which cooperative endeavor among individuals is carried forward in a social system. Unconsciously, we rebel at the idea of ourselves in a slave or serf culture, and we refuse, again unconsciously, to face up to the reality that, in fact, many of our relationships with our fellows are political in the Tullockian sense. Only this blindness to reality can explain the failure of modern scholars to have developed a more satisfactory theory of individual behavior in hierarchic structures. This also explains why Tullock has found it necessary to go to the Eastern literature and to the discussions in earlier historical epochs for comparative analysis.

Traditional economic analysis can be helpful in illustrating this fundamental distinction between the economic and the political relationship. A seller is in a purely economic relationship with his buyers when he confronts a number of them, any one of which is prepared to purchase his commodity or service at the established market price. He is a slave to no single buyer, and he need "please" no one provided only that he performs the task for which he contracts, that he "delivers the goods." By contrast, consider the seller who confronts a single buyer with no alternative buyer existent. In this case, the relationship becomes wholly "political." The price becomes exclusively that which the economist calls "pure rent" since, by hypothesis, the seller has no alternative use to which he can put his commodity or service. He is, thus, at the absolute mercy of the single buyer. He is, in fact, a "slave" to this buyer, and he must "please" in order to secure favorable terms, in order to advance his own welfare. Note here that the domestic servant who contracts "to please" a buyer of his services may, in fact, remain in a predominantly economic relationship if a sufficient number of alternative buyers for his services exist whereas the corporation executive who supervises a sizable

number of people may be in a predominantly political relationship with his own superior. To the economist, Tullock
provides a discussion of the origins of economic rent, and a
theory of the relationship between the recipient and the
donor of economic rent.

Tullock's distinction here can also be useful in discussing
an age-old philosophical dilemma. When is a man confronted with a free choice? The traveler's choice between
giving up his purse and death, as offered to him by the high-
wayman, is, in reality, no choice at all. Yet philosophers
have found it difficult to define explicitly the line that divides
situations into categories of free and unfree or coerced
choices. One approach to a possible classification here lies
in the extent to which individual response to an apparent
choice situation might be predicted by an external observer.
If, in fact, the specific action of the individual, confronted
with an apparent choice, is predictable within narrow limits,
no effective choosing or deciding process could take place.
By comparison, if the individual response is not predictable
with a high degree of probability, choice can be defined as
being effectively free. By implication, Tullock's analysis
would suggest that individual action in a political relationship might be somewhat more predictable than individual
action in the economic relationship because of the simple
fact that, in the latter, there exist alternatives. If this implication is correctly drawn, the possibilities of developing a
predictive "science" of "politics" would seem to be inher-
ently greater than those of developing a science of economics. Yet we observe, of course, that economic theory
has an established and legitimate claim to the position as
being the only social science with genuine predictive value.
The apparent paradox here is explained by the generality

with which the economist can apply his criteria for measuring the results of individual choice. Through his ability to bring many results within the "measuring rod of money," the economist is able to make reasonably accurate predictions about the behavior of "average" or "representative" men; behavior that, in individual cases, stems from unconstrained, or free, choices. Only through this possibility of relying on representative individuals can economics be a predictive science; predictions about the behavior of individually identifiable human beings are clearly impossible except in rare instances. By contrast, because his choice is less free, the behavior of the individual politician in a bureaucratic hierarchy can be predicted with somewhat greater accuracy than the behavior of the individual in the marketplace. But there exist no general, quantitatively measurable, criteria that will allow the external observer to test hypotheses about political behavior. There exists no measuring rod for bureaucratic advancement comparable to the economist's money scale. For these reasons, hypotheses about individual behavior are more important in Tullock's analysis, and the absence of external variables that are subject to quantification makes the refutation of positive hypotheses difficult in the extreme. For assistance here, Tullock introduces a simple, but neglected, method. He asks the reader whether or not his own experience leads him to accept or to reject the hypotheses concerning the behavior of the politician in bureaucracy.

Tullock makes no attempt to conceal from view his opinion that large hierarchical structures are, with certain explicit exceptions, unnecessary evils, that these are not appropriate parts of the good society. A unique value of the book lies, however, in the fact that this becomes more than mere opinion, more than mere expression of personal value judgments. The emphasis is properly placed on the need for greater scientific analysis. Far too often social scientists have, I fear, introduced explicit value judgments before analysis should have ceased. Ultimately, of course, discussion must reduce to values, but when it does so it is done. If the indolent scholar relies on an appeal to values at the outset, his role in genuine discussion is, almost by definition, eliminated.

The bureaucratic world that Tullock pictures for us is not an attractive one, even when its abstract character is recognized, and even if the reference politician of that world is not assigned the dominant role in real life. Those of us who accept the essential ethics of the free society find this world difficult to think about, much less to discuss critically and to evaluate. External events, however, force us to the realization that this is, to a large extent, the world in which we now live. The ideal society of freely contracting "equals," always a noble fiction, has, for all practical purposes, disappeared even as a norm in this age of increasing collectivization: political, economic, and philosophical.

Faced with this reality, the libertarian need not despair. The technology of the twentieth century has made small organizations inefficient in many respects, and the Jeffersonian image of the free society can never be realized. However, just as the critics of the laissez-faire economic order were successful in their efforts to undermine the public faith in the functioning of the invisible hand, the new critics of the emerging bureaucratic order can be successful in undermining an equally naive faith in the benevolence of governmental bureaucracy. Tullock's analysis, above all else, arouses the reader to an awareness of the inefficiencies of large hierarchical structures, independently of the presumed purposes or objectives of these organizations. The benevolent despot image of government, that seems now to exist in the minds of so many men, is effectively shattered.

Genuine progress toward the reform of social institutions becomes possible when man learns that the ideal order of affairs is neither the laissez-faire dream of Herbert Spencer nor the benevolent despotism image. Man in the West, as well as in the East, must learn that governments, even governments by the people, can do so many things poorly, and many things not at all. If this very simple fact could be more widely recognized by the public at large (the ultimate sovereign in any society over the long run), a genuinely free society of individuals and groups might again become a realizable goal for the organization of man's cooperative endeavors. We do not yet know the structure of this society, and we may have to grope our way along for decades. Surely and certainly, however, man must cling to that uniquely important discovery of modern history, the discovery of man, the individual human being. If we abandon or forget this discovery, and allow ourselves to be drawn along any one of the many roads to serfdom by false gods, we do not deserve to survive.

9

Notes on the History and Direction of Public Choice

B y way of introduction, I call your attention to two papers. The first is Scott Gordon's, "The New Contractarians,"[1] which was an extended review article on Rawls,
Nozick, and Buchanan. The second is Milton Friedman's
Nobel Prize lecture, "Inflation and Unemployment."[2] In
the former, Gordon accused me of committing the "natu-
ralistic fallacy," that of deriving an "ought" from an "is,"
of mixing positive analysis and normative precept. In the
latter, Friedman argues that economics is, after all, a "science" like the natural sciences in the sense that it develops
through the refutation of hypotheses.

You may appropriately ask what has all this to do with
my title. Let me try to explain. I was not particularly disturbed by Gordon's accusation, since I have never worried
very much about whether or not my own work falls within
the methodological precepts laid down by others. I viewed

This chapter was initially prepared for panel presentation at the Public
Choice Society Meeting, New Orleans, March 11, 1977.
[1] Scott Gordon, "The New Contractarians," *Journal of Political Economy*
84, no. 3 (June 1976): 573–75.
[2] Nobel Foundation, December 1976.

my book *The Limits of Liberty*[3] as basically positive analysis, with ethical content squeezed to a minimum. I did not want explicitly to advance my own private values; I did not want to spell out, and I refrained from doing so, just how society "ought" to be organized. I think that my values count for no more in this respect than anyone else's. But we must all recognize, I think, that the ultimate purpose of positive analysis, conceptual or empirical, must be that of modifying the environment for choices, which must, in some basic sense, be normatively informed. The ultimate purpose is the "ought," no matter how purely we stick positively with the "is." Or to put a familiar statement of Pigou in context here, in social sciences it is the heat we are looking for, not pure light.

Let me take a single economics and public-choice example, the federal minimum-wage laws. Economists are almost universally agreed that the requirement of the uniform minimum wage creates a good part of the observed unemployment among teenagers, and notably teenaged members of minority groups (Ray Marshall to the contrary notwithstanding; Marshall really disqualifies himself as an economist by his position on such matters). This relationship between minimum wages and unemployment is perhaps as well established, both analytically and empirically, as any in the whole discipline of economics. But we do not observe some mysterious leap from this demonstrated "is" to the "ought" of the repeal of these restrictions. Why not? Public-choice analysts have provided part of the answer. They have looked straightforwardly at the self-interested motivations of certain groups in maintaining the minimum wage.

---

[3] Chicago: University of Chicago Press, 1975.

Whereas many economists, locked in normatively to their notions of efficiency, would be quite willing to infer an "ought" from the "is" relationship here, public-choice theory allows us to demonstrate the future "is" proposition that explains why elected politicians pay so little attention to the economists' urgings. There is disagreement on the "ought" because the maintenance of the uniform minimum wage is to the interest of large groups of voters. And we are left with the "is" of observed policy, without a means of crossing the bridge to the "ought."

I shall return to this point later, but first let me trace out a bit of the "history" part of my remarks. Duncan Black was correct in labeling his theory one of "committees and elections" rather than a theory of democratic or governmental process. A small number of persons choosing among a small number of discrete alternatives—this is the idealized setting for the analysis of simple voting rules, surely one central part of public-choice theory as it has developed to date. But public-choice theorists have, perhaps too readily, transferred this analysis to the complex setting of political reality, where a few "candidates" become many "issues," where "issues" are prepackaged in platforms, where electorates number in the millions, and where there may be little correspondence between the simple choices confronted by the voter and the outcomes that may occur. The deficiencies of the demand-driven models of government, of an essentially passive supplier of public goods and services responding to the demands of median preferences—these deficiencies have come to be increasingly apparent, both because of our observations of real-world political behavior and because of analytical contributions represented in the theories of bureaucracy and application of monopoly models to governments. Increasingly, public-choice theorists now find common ground with some of the early Italian theorists who worked with ruling-class or establishment models of the state. The Leviathan that we observe today simply cannot be ignored.

In oversimplified terms we can look at the history of public-choice theory in this two-stage manner. First, there was the working out of voting-rule theory under demand-driven models of governmental process. Second, there was, and is, the working out of theories of transmission via organizational structures of government. In both stages, however, we can summarize public choice as a theory of "governmental failure," at least by comparison with the public-interest image inherent in the Wilsonian-Weberian conception of bureaucracy and the "truth-judgment" image of politics that informed so much of traditional pre-public-choice political science. Public choice is a theory of "governmental failure" here in the precisely analogous sense that theoretical welfare economics has been a theory of "market failure."

Let me return to Friedman's Nobel Prize lecture and to the "ought-is" question raised by Scott Gordon. Friedman suggests, implicitly, if not explicitly, that "science" is all, that the refutation of hypotheses is all that we are required to do, that a demonstration of the "is" must necessarily lead to some consensus on the "ought." Applied to the development of positive public-choice theory, the Friedman message is clear. By means of widely accepted demonstrations, both analytical and empirical, that governmental processes "fail" by comparison with alternative arrangements, our task is largely complete. The policy implications will, presumably, emerge from the "scientific advance" more or less automatically even if somehow mysteriously.

I suppose that my rejection of this view is evident. The "ought" of policy does not follow from the "is" of positive science in economics or in politics. I am on Hobbes' side of the argument here as in so many other places, for I recall that Hobbes is alleged to have stated that we should never have accepted the "truth" that two plus two equals four if it had been to the interest of any group to oppose this logic of the simple number system. To bring us forward more than three centuries to a 1977 example, can anything be more demonstrably self-evident than the superiority of the aggregate benefits of the TVA Tellico dam over the costs of eliminating the snail darter, which my informed biologist colleagues tell me is not an endangered species anyway? I hope that we shall not be so naive as to think that, because we have made progress toward some understanding of the way governmental processes actually function, improvements in design will follow, more or less as a matter of course. Would it were so!

Which brings me directly to what I have to say about the future developments and direction of public choice. Put bluntly, I think that we must become more *normative* in our efforts; we should use the results of our positive analysis in the discussion of policy reform. We must use the "is" to implement the "ought" which the "is" suggests, regardless of the methodological impropriety of this relationship, Scott Gordon to the contrary notwithstanding.

But let me clarify my position here. I am not, repeat not, proposing that we dirty our hands in day-to-day policy advocacy of the Brookings variety. I shall leave that to the

Joe Pechmans of the world, although I do sometimes get a bit concerned about the one-sided progovernment, proregulation biases in such representation. But this aside, the sort of normative public choice that I support is far from such direct policy advocacy.

Again let me use an example. Public-choice analysts have no business telling President Carter or Jim Schlesinger just what energy policy "ought" to be proposed. Nor do they even have any role in delineating what would be an "ideal" policy mix. Positive public-choice analysts can tell us, however, and within broad limits, roughly the sort of energy policy that is likely to emerge from the collective decision-making institutions that we observe in operation. This is, and has been, our major contribution. And our predictions can tell us that the emergent results are unlikely to bear much relationship to those results desired, even by those who make the final normative decision as to the "ought." In a sense, public-choice analysts can take on a normative role in advocating some matching of policy proposals with the institutional realities of modern politics. We can talk meaningfully about the "best" rules, or the "nth best" arrangements, often quite independently of the ultimate policy targets. In other words, we can talk normatively about "process" or "procedure," while staying clear of normative discussion of "end-states."

Perhaps I should go further and say that public-choice theorists should begin to advance their own versions of the ideal constitution for society. In this, I may be doing nothing more than suggesting the way in which my own directions seem to lie rather than inferring this for the whole of the public-choice subdiscipline. But let me extend these remarks only a bit more to constitutionalism. I have argued, along with others, that we must have a genuine constitutional dialogue, and soon, if America is to remain a free society, if we are to escape the ravages of Rome (with some parallels forcefully brought home to me in a recent manuscript by Professor Silver)[4] and the British disease of our own century. There is still time. It is folly to think that "better men" elected to office will help us much, that "better policy" will turn things around here. We need, and must have, basic constitutional reform, which must of course be preceded by basic constitutional discourse and discussion. This is our challenge.

Public choice can claim to have contributed hugely to what can be the basis for such discourse and discussion. But there is also room for, indeed a necessity for, some intellectual entrepreneurship, some normative advocacy, in getting the dialogue going. The "science" does not create its own consequences.

Let us continue to scorn the petty bickerings of the partisan policy advocates; we should not be bothered at all as to whether or not mortgage interest is or is not a tax deduction, and we waste our time thinking about such matters. We should care, and we should think about, what the fiscal constitution for political democracy should look like, what sort of institutions should be most efficient in the workings of democratic politics. But we must do more than analyze what is. If we do not go beyond this, if we do not begin to suggest explicitly what "ought to be" in terms of these basic constitutional reforms of process, we can scarcely complain when we observe the continued drift into constitutional

---

[4] Morris Silver, "Decline of Affluent Societies," mimeographed (New York: City College of the City University of New York, 1977).

chaos. The several prisoners caught in a dilemma may all recognize their plight; but before escape is possible someone must take the step of changing his own behavior in an attempt to convince others that all can be made better off in the process.

In the final analysis, I refuse to think everything is hopeless, which strictly positive analysis without the accompanying Friedman faith might lead us to believe.

10

Public Choice
and Public Finance

In an earlier survey paper, "Public Finance and Public
Choice,"[1] I traced the developments in American public
finance in the years after World War II, and I demonstrated
how the emergence of public-choice theory has been influ-
ential in affecting these developments. To an extent, my
discussion in this paper must parallel that of my earlier
effort. I shall, however, emphasize somewhat different
points here. I shall first briefly discuss the public-finance
origins of public-choice theory. I shall argue that public
finance is, indeed, the parent discipline out of which the
more generally applicable public-choice theory, now sometimes called the "economic theory of politics," emerged. Following this introductory look at the origins, my two main
sections concentrate on the effects of public-choice theory
on positive and normative public finance. I shall show how
the introduction of public choice dramatically expands the
scope for positive analysis and how it shifts the focus for

This chapter was initially prepared for presentation at the Thirty-fourth
Congress, International Institute of Public Finance, Hamburg, Germany,
September 4–8, 1978.

[1] *National Tax Journal* 28 (December 1975): 383–94.

normative understanding and evaluation of fiscal institutions. In the discussion of these two main sections, several public-finance applications of public-choice theory will be mentioned, along with what seem to me to be promising directions for research.

The Public-Finance Origins of
Public-Choice Theory

"Public finance" is about taxing and spending. Both of these are activities rather of governments or collectivities than of individuals as private persons. This feature alone distinguishes public finance from the other traditional subdisciplines in economics, those which concentrate largely if not entirely on the activities of nongovernmental decision-makers, on the behavior of consumers, producers, entrepreneurs, workers, etc. Viewed in this basic perspective, it would seem neither surprising nor inappropriate that, in the European tradition, public finance should have occupied a position related more closely to law than to economic theory. There is no cause for wonderment, therefore, in the fact that the important precursors of modern public-choice theory are to be found among the works of those economists who were trained within the European public-finance tradition. In a summary definition, public choice is the analysis of political decision-making with the tools and methods of economics. For specific precursors, we look to the works of Continental scholars like Sax, Mazzola, Pantaleoni, De Viti, De Marco, and, most important, Knut Wicksell, all of whom wrote before the end of the nineteenth century. The works of these scholars differed substantially one from another, but all shared a common objective, which was to bring the public economy within the analytical framework that had seemed so successful in explaining the working of the private economy. To do this, these scholars almost necessarily were forced to pay some attention to the political decision structure within which taxing and spending choices were made.

It is interesting to speculate on why these seminal works were so much neglected for half a century, especially in Britain and America, but also to an extent on the Continent itself, only to be "rediscovered" and extended in the decades since World War II, not only in public-choice theory strictly defined but also in the theory of public goods. The unproductive state of classical political economy, Benthamite utilitarianism, and idealist political philosophy—these may be introduced as partial causes for the British neglect of the Continental literature. But the mystery remains: Why were economists generally so slow in extending their basic tools of analysis to the behavior of persons who act in public-choice rather than in private-choice capacities?

It is not surprising that several scholars who made early contributions in public-choice theory came to the subdiscipline by way of public-finance theory, and, for the most part, reflected some influence of the Continental writings mentioned. Duncan Black and I both provide good examples. Black's first book was on the incidence of income taxes, strictly within the subject matter of traditional public finance. But Black read the Italian writers in public finance, and he also read Wicksell. From this background emerged his now classic work on the theory of committees, which, of course, has general applicability extending much beyond public-finance problems. In my own case, I was trained initially as a standard public-finance economist, but a chance reading of Wicksell, followed by an examination of the Italian works, turned my attention increasingly to analysis of political decision structures, to constitutional rules, and away from the set of problems in public-finance orthodoxy. I found myself less interested in the old question, How should tax shares be allocated? and at the same time more interested in the new question, How are tax shares allocated in a democracy? There seemed to me to be little value or purpose in normative discourse about optimal or efficient taxation until we achieved a better understanding of how political structures produce fiscal outcomes. In my case, I was not specifically motivated by the scientific superiority of this sort of positive analysis over the normative discussion of the traditional question.

The Expanded Domain for Positive Analysis in Public Finance

The positive-normative dichotomy does, however, provide a useful way of classifying the impact of public choice on public finance. One of the most important effects has been that of expanding the domain for positive analysis in public finance. Public choice opens up new sets of questions to be asked; the subject matter of the discipline has been dramatically increased. It will be useful to be quite specific on this point. Several categories of positive analysis may be distinguished.

1. The Effects of Alternative Fiscal Institutions, Existing and Potential, on the Behavior of Persons and Groups in the Private Economy, in *Private Choice*.

This category offered the *only* domain for positive economic analysis in post-Marshallian public finance in the

English-language tradition. Even when broadly defined, this category includes essentially the theory of shifting and incidence, applied to taxes and to public outlays. As such, and as Marshall himself recognized and noted, the subject matter is applied price theory, which is precisely where it was located in American doctoral curricula before World War II. Comparative statistics offered a plausible predictive framework for analyzing the effects of alternative tax arrangements. Within limits, the economist could predict how particular taxes would affect the behavior of persons in the market economy, and through this could predict aggregate effects on such variables as relative prices, outputs, profits, and industry structures. This positive analysis also enabled the economist to derive empirically refutable propositions. Restricted to these questions, the public-finance economist had little reason to extend his inquiry to the purposes of taxation and public outlay.

Research in this traditional area of positive public finance has continued to be developed through more sophisticated analytical techniques in the decades since World War II. Work has moved beyond the Marshallian partial equilibrium framework into general equilibrium settings, including the extension of analysis from a closed to an open economy. The area of inquiry remains important; the hard questions in incidence theory have not all been resolved, and these will continue to command the attention of economists. What public choice has done is to remove this area of analysis from its position of exclusive dominance in positive public finance. Other significant and equally legitimate applications of positive economic analysis have been opened up, areas of inquiry that were foreclosed in the Marshallian regime.

2. The Effects of Alternative Fiscal Institutions, Existing and Potential, on the Behavior of Persons and Groups in the Public Economy, *in Public Choice.*

If the effects of a designated fiscal institution—say, a specific excise tax—on the behavior of persons in private markets may be analyzed, what is to deter the intellectually curious economist from examining the effects of this tax on the behavior of persons in "public markets"? If persons pay for public goods through such a tax, might they not be predicted to "purchase" or to "demand" differing quantities from those that they would demand under alternative financing schemes? Once such questions are raised, the need for answers, along with the opportunities for productive analytical and empirical research, seems self-evident. An implicit and unquestioned assumption to the effect that the level and the composition of budgetary outlays must remain invariant under widely differing tax arrangements surely cannot be either analytically or empirically legitimate.

The whole set of questions here stems from the "publicness" of the goods and services as these are demanded and consumed and as these are supplied through political or governmental institutions. Individuals do not pay "prices" for partitionable units of these goods. They pay "taxes," which are coercively imposed through a political process, and this coercion is, in turn, made necessary by the free-rider motivation inherent in general collective action. Few persons will voluntarily pay taxes if they expect to receive the benefits from generally available public goods. But what quantity will persons, when they act collectively in public-choice capacities—as voters, actual or potential, as government employees—choose to provide and to finance? This choice depends on the bridge that is constructed between the benefits or spending side of the fiscal account and the costs or taxing side. Differing fiscal arrangements, different tax rules, will influence the weighing of these accounts. What are the implications for budgetary levels if taxes are spread more generally than benefits? And vice versa? Will more or fewer public goods be generated under a regime of indirect taxation or under one of direct taxation? Will the number of tax sources influence the size of the budget? Fiscal perception becomes an important and relevant part of positive analysis in public finance. By necessity what has sometimes been called "fiscal psychology" merges with fiscal economics.

This area of inquiry remains perhaps less well developed than any other in positive public finance, and the potential for productive research seems almost unlimited.[2] But there is a significant methodological block to be surmounted here, one that warrants brief discussion. Tradition-bound economists react negatively to the notion that individuals may be influenced in their choice behavior by institutional structure. Economists are prone to extend their postulate of individual rationality to include the ability of persons to "see through" the institutional maze and to reject attempts to explain patterns of outcomes by resort to such things as "fiscal illusion," that institutions may be alleged to create. In my view, this attitude is based on a failure to appreciate the differing analytical settings for market and for public choice. In ordinary markets, the presumption that all persons choose rationally does little to distort empirical reality because the rationality of only a few participants who can

---

[2] My own book, *Public Finance in Democratic Process* (Chapel Hill: University of North Carolina Press, 1967), is largely a call for such research, along with a summary of some initial efforts.

affect results at the appropriate margins of adjustment guarantees the equivalence of outcomes as between what we might call the full rationality and the partial rationality models. The situation in "public markets" is not at all analogous. Solutions do not emerge as the outcome of the mutual interactions of many participants who make private and independent decisions. Instead, public-market solutions are the result of the interactions of many persons who are necessarily involved in the unique public or collective decision. The result reflects the choice of the median voter, or his representative, who may or may not be fully rational in the sense that informs traditional price theory. The presumption of fully informed rationality here is much more severely restrictive than in any other market setting. Fiscal economists should not be deterred by methodological criticism that is essentially without foundation from going ahead in research efforts to find out just how differing fiscal structures might indeed affect the information and perceptions of the relevant public choosers.

3. The Effects of Alternative Political or Collective-Choice Institutions, Existing or Potential, on the Behavior of Persons and Groups in the Public Economy, *in Public Choice*.

This area of positive inquiry is related to, but quite different from, that discussed above, and this area is more central to what might be termed "public-choice theory" in the narrow sense. Analysis here involves the working properties of the choice-making institutions themselves, as these might be predicted to generate taxing and spending results. Research here involves the public-finance applications of the theory of voting.

What budget characteristics can be predicted to emerge under the operation of simple majority voting rules? What difference in the size and composition of outlays might emerge when general-fund budgeting is compared with separate-purpose budgeting, with earmarked tax sources? What differences in the willingness to issue public debt can be predicted when the effective voting franchise is expanded from local property owners to all members of the electorate? What will be the comparative levels of public spending on, say, education, when these services are provided through a set of monopoly school districts and through the market response to educational vouchers supplied directly to families? What are the effects of school-district consolidation on budget size and quality of service? What are the effects of franchising bureaucrats on the level and the growth of public spending?

These are only a few of the questions that have been, and might be, asked by those who approach public finance from the generalized public-choice paradigm. As these sample questions suggest, the domain for positive analysis here includes institutional analysis at a level where explanatory hypotheses are derived deductively from abstract models, and also at a level where the implications of these hypotheses may be tested empirically.[3]

The Modified Domain for Normative Public Finance

As the above discussion suggests, public choice has expanded the domain for positive analysis in public finance. But what about the domain for normative discourse? Here,

---

[3] Some of the early applications are contained in the separate papers included in the volume *Theory of Public Choice*, ed. James M. Buchanan and Robert Tollison (Ann Arbor: University of Michigan Press, 1972). For a textbook that employs a fiscal-choice paradigm, see Richard E. Wagner, *The Public Economy* (Chicago: Markham, 1973).

too, the effects of public choice are both interesting and important. As I shall demonstrate, these effects serve, in one sense, to restore legitimacy to much of the age-old discussions in normative tax theory, a legitimacy that seems absent in the public-finance extension of the norms from theoretical welfare economics.

It will be useful to commence with the latter, which may be summarized under the rubric "theory of public goods." This development, like public-choice theory, has roots in the Continental tradition, but for my narrative summary it will be useful to start with Samuelson's seminal formulation in 1954.[4] He posed the normative question: What are the necessary conditions for efficiency that must be satisfied in the public economy? Having defined these conditions in aggregative terms, Samuelson turned to a "social welfare function" to determine the final distribution of welfare among persons net of the public-goods production and subsequent benefits. There is no scope for normative tax theory, as such, in this basic Samuelson model.

Less general norms for the marginal imputation of tax shares are found in the earlier model developed by Erik Lindahl, norms which also meet the Samuelson allocative requirements. The concept of Lindahl equilibrium in the public economy has emerged to command the attention of general equilibrium theorists in the last decade, and notably those theorists who are primarily interested in establishing existence proofs and in assessing stability properties of solutions. Given an initial set of endowments, and extending the Lindahl imputation of marginal tax shares over infra-

---

[4] Paul A. Samuelson, "The Pure Theory of Public Expenditure," *Review of Economics and Statistics* 36 (November 1954): 387–89.

marginal ranges for individual quantity evaluation, the allocation of tax payments among persons becomes unique in the Lindahl solution. Once this allocation is formally defined, there is once again no scope for normative tax theory in terms of relative evaluations of traditional tax instruments.

The traditional questions in normative tax theory have, however, witnessed something of a modern revival, beyond the limits of either general equilibrium welfare theory or public-choice theory. I refer here to the work in "optimal taxation," which has come to occupy the attention of several competent young practitioners in public finance during the 1970s. In a very general sense, this work examines the old questions of normative public finance with the sophisticated tools of modern mathematical economics. Those who have worked in this area have been willing to look at the allocation of tax shares independently of globally efficient solutions to the fiscal process; they have been ready to ignore the efficiency norms derivative from the theory of public goods. Hence, despite its sophistication in technique, "optimal tax theory" is something of a methodological throwback to the pre-Wicksellian framework of Anglo-American public finance.

So much for a hurried, and necessarily incomplete, discussion of normative public finance as it stands today, independent from and outside the normative domain that is offered in the context of the public-choice paradigm. Let me now turn to the question as to how public-choice theory has changed and can change the whole setting for normative analysis in public finance.

My answer claims a great deal for public choice, but I think that its potential for productive normative work can scarcely be overly estimated. Properly introduced and interpreted, the public-choice paradigm enables us to combine the logical realism of Wicksell with the obvious political relevance of some of the traditional questions that normative tax theory has addressed.

In any community in which the government is not wholly divorced from the citizenry, the fiscal process must logically be modeled as a two-sided exchange. Taxes are payments made for benefits received. But how is it possible to envisage the collective-choice process, in the context of observed political structures, as a positive-sum game? How can we model the participation by individuals in the complex network out of which taxing and spending results finally emerge?

Here we must return directly to Wicksell, to look at his basic insights along with his normative arguments. Wicksell was interested in reform, and he recognized the essential absurdity of proffering normative advice on the assumption that some benevolent despot would listen. Wicksell stressed that fiscal results emerge from political institutions, and that if reform was to be introduced, the institutional structure must be modified. He recognized, further, that there was some substitutability between the institutions for making political choices and those for taxing and spending. As we know, he aimed most of his normative argument at political structure. He was quite willing to relax many of the rigidities of tax rules in exchange for efficiency-increasing changes in political decision rules.

In one sense, we may say that the normative public-finance implications of public-choice theory involve the other half of this Wicksellian duality. In the context of established political institutions, how can fiscal institutions be modified so as to produce more acceptable results? How can the taxing and spending *process* be improved? This is the normative issue to be addressed, as opposed to the more direct, but also empty, issue concerning specific allocations of outlays and of tax shares.

Empirically, we observe individuals, in their public-choice capacities as voters, politicians, bureaucrats, choosing, not among tax-share allocations in each period, but among alternative tax institutions that, as they operate, will produce tax-share distributions as a result. Legislatures choose among alternative financing instruments—among such instruments as personal income taxation, progressive or proportional in rates, corporate or company taxation, turnover taxation, commodity taxation, wealth taxation, etc. In real-world settings, tax arrangements or rules, once these are settled, are expected to remain in place for a long succession of budgetary periods, in each one of which outlay allocations are made. The choice among tax institutions is, properly considered, analogous to the choice among rules, or to *constitutional* choice.

Once we begin to think of the choice among tax arrangements in constitutional terms, however, we escape the zero-sum implications that tax-share imputation in any single budgetary period necessarily invokes. It becomes conceptually possible to think about tax-sharing arrangements, which could never be accepted by all persons in the community in a single-period context, as commanding consensus at some prior constitutional stage of deliberation and argument. It becomes possible to establish criteria for potential agreement on tax institutions, including some of those that we have historically observed, in a constitutional or contractual setting. At least ideally, it is now possible to derive norms for the fiscal structure that are internal to the utility functions of the members of the community and not externally drawn from ethical principles.

I am not suggesting that the constitutional approach which the public-choice paradigm implies necessarily removes all elements of interpersonal or intergroup conflict from tax-share allocation. But the analysis does allow departure from the pure conflict model that orthodox normative theory must introduce. The question becomes: What is the structure of taxation upon which individuals might agree at some constitutional stage, in the knowledge that, once implemented, this structure is to remain in force over a succession of periods? To establish some sort of contractual agreement here, the quasi-permanency of the institutions is necessary, since only in this way can the necessary uncertainty be introduced regarding the identity of individual economic status. In the limit, the potential taxpayer-beneficiary, asked to participate in the constitutional selection process, is behind a complete veil of ignorance as regards his own future position.[5]

I shall not try here to elaborate on this constitutional approach to normative public-finance theory. I hope that my cursory comments have been able to suggest that exciting work remains to be done. I am currently working on what we call the "tax constitution," or, more broadly, the "fiscal

---

[5] In our book *The Calculus of Consent* (Ann Arbor: University of Michigan Press, 1962), Gordon Tullock and I used the quasi-permanency of constitutional rules as a means of introducing the uncertainty necessary to produce agreement on rules. In his more general, and more explicitly normative, discussion of principles of justice, John Rawls invokes the veil of ignorance which all persons face in the original position, before basic social institutions are settled (Rawls, *A Theory of Justice* [Cambridge, Mass.: Harvard University Press, 1971]).

constitution" for a community under specific assumptions about the workings of the political process. This research has already yielded results that turn much of the traditional normative theory on its head. I shall not summarize this research here. But I should note only that it is necessary to call on the positive analysis from each of the three separate areas of inquiry listed above before any attempt is made to derive plausibly acceptable norms for fiscal reform. We must know or at least make some predictions about who bears the burden of taxes. We must know or at least make some predictions about how various taxes affect public as well as private choices. We must know or at least make some predictions about how political processes work. Only then can we even begin to ask questions about justice in taxation, the ultimate normative issue. Wicksell called his treatise a new principle for justice in taxation. Public-choice theory can, following his lead, help in the elaboration of the Wicksellian precepts.

Part Three

Economics as
Moral Philosophy

11

Methods and Morals in Economics

Introduction

My initial reaction to the 1935 discussion between C. E. Ayres and Frank H. Knight is one of vivid contrast between the economist's intellectual world of 1935 and that of the 1970s.[1] Ayres and Knight, leading members of the profession, explicitly concerned themselves with fundamental philosophical issues that emerge naturally from the discipline. By comparison, how many economists in the 1970s debate similar issues or, what is more critical, so much as recognize that they exist? Surely the basic problems have not been resolved, despite the developments, good and bad, that have resulted from the Robbins, the Robinson-Chamberlin, and the Keynesian "revolutions." These issues have only taken different form, as affected by forty years of additional history.

This chapter was initially published in *Science and Ceremony*, ed. William Breit and W. P. Culbertson (Austin: University of Texas Press, 1976), pp. 163–74. Permission to reprint is herewith acknowledged.

[1] C. E. Ayres, "Moral Confusion in Economics," *International Journal of Ethics* (January 1935): 170–99; Frank H. Knight, "Intellectual Confusion in Morals and Economics," *International Journal of Ethics* (January 1935): 200–220; Ayres, "Confusion Thrice Confounded," *International Journal of Ethics* (April 1935): 356–58.

In this chapter, I propose to present the 1935 Ayres-Knight discussion in modern dress, so to speak. I shall argue that developments in economics since 1935 have been such as to bring their positions more closely into agreement, although both continue to be sharply divergent from mainstream economic methodology. Both of these scholars should have become increasingly disturbed at the increasing mathematization of economic theory, quite independently of the uses to which this might have been put. By "mathematization" here I refer to the conceptualization of economics as a branch of applied mathematics. Both scholars should have been equally if not more disturbed by the emergence of the dominating professional emphasis on empirical testing of hypotheses, themselves grounded in idealized theoretical constructions, as if the interaction of human beings in society were fully equivalent to the interaction of chemical elements. Ayres might have been at least ambivalent with respect to developments in theoretical welfare economics, properly characterized as "theories of market failure." This might have been matched by Knight's ambivalence toward developments in public-choice theory, which could be dubbed "theories of government failure." Both Ayres and Knight would have continued to emphasize the limits to the explanatory potential of purely economic models of man, and both might have maintained their interests in exploring the moral-ethical requirements for social order, requirements that must be met before effective economic interaction begins.

Theory of Social Order

As we read the 1935 discussion between Clarence Ayres and Frank Knight, their differences emerge; their points of agreement tend to be obscured because these were mutually acknowledged by the participants. This is perhaps most clearly demonstrated by Knight's silence on Ayres' insistence that the function of economics is to offer a theory of social order, of social interaction. "Of course," Knight would have responded here, and students at the University of Chicago, before and after 1935, placed this theory at the core of Knight's teaching. Modern, post-1935, developments make this elementary methodological principle worthy of reemphasis. By saying that economics offers or should offer a theory of social order, we must, by direct implication, say that economics is not exclusively or even primarily a "theory of choice."[2] Yet the thrust of post-1935 development, influenced perhaps too strongly by Robbins' *Nature and Significance of Economic Science*,[3] has surely been toward the latter rather than the former. Once we accept the Robbins formulation of the "economic problem," we are, almost necessarily, forced into a choice-theoretic framework, and the tools of applied mathematics suggest themselves immediately. Economics comes to be conceptualized as a varied set of exercises, all of which involve the maximization of some appropriately selected objective function subject to the appropriately defined constraints, with, of course, the dual minimization problems always offering alternative avenues toward solutions. Formally, the problem faced by the isolated Robinson Crusoe is no different from that facing the political community of persons. Once

[2] For an elaboration of my own position, see my paper, "Is Economics the Science of Choice?" in *Roads to Freedom: Essays in Honor of F. A. Hayek*, ed. E. Streissler (London: Routledge & Kegan Paul, 1969), pp. 47–64. Reprinted in this book as chapter two.

[3] Lionel Robbins, *The Nature and Significance of Economic Science* (London: Macmillan, 1932).

a utility function is specified and its constraints defined, the economist observer can tell Crusoe just what his "efficient" pattern of behavior must be. Once a "social welfare function" is specified and the constraints are known, the same observer can tell the benevolent despot just how the whole economy must be "efficiently" organized and operated. The role of the economist shifts readily and almost imperceptibly from that of the disinterested "engineer" to that of normative counselor, proffering his own judgmental advice as to ends as well as means, if in fact these can ever be separated.

There is a subtle, but vitally important, distinction between this choice-theoretic approach and that which is properly attributable to the theorist of social interaction. In the latter, Robinson Crusoe economics continues to occupy a place, but never one embracing the conceptual or imagined purpose of proffering advice and counsel. We seek to understand Crusoe's isolated behavior as a first and preliminary conceptual stage in understanding the emergent interrelationships among men as they meet in socioeconomic processes. The focus of attention is upon "that which tends to emerge" from the behavioral interaction, and this is not conceptualized as a "solution" to any applied maximization problem faced by some representation or idealization of the whole community of participants. Economists, as specialists, describe characteristics of these results, but it is the structural-procedural aspects that command attention, never the results as such. To introduce a simple example from the Crusoe-Friday world, the economist is unconcerned as to whether the established trading ratio between coconuts and fish settles at $5:1$, $1:1$, or $1:5$. He does not view the exchange process as an "analogue computing device" that makes "choices" for the idealized community. His concern is devoted to the demonstration that in idealized conditions of exchange the trading process ensures an equality among the internal trading ratios for all participants.

I am not suggesting here that either Frank Knight or Clarence Ayres fully articulated and consistently held the second position that I have outlined. Through Knight's insistence on the central role of the equimarginal or "economic" principle, even in the multiperson setting, Knight's work is, of course, fully consistent with and can readily be interpreted as falling within the broad choice-theoretic framework. By his query, "Are we going on the rocks?" repeatedly made in his 1935 essay, Ayres implies that he viewed the social economy in a "ship of state" analogue, one which readily translates into "social welfare function" notation. Had he used a slightly different metaphor, he might have ventured a more appropriate question for a theorist of social order. Had he asked, "Is the island sinking?" he would have implied thereby a potential disintegration or breakdown in the institutional foundations of society, within which human interaction takes place and from which outcomes emerge, but outcomes that are not purposefully directed by any single choosing agent. Nonetheless, I should argue that both men equally would view as essentially absurd modern attempts to "compute" equilibrium prices along with both the expressed hopes and fears that advanced computer technology can replace exchange processes or, more generally, can essentially remove human actors from society.

Homo Economicus

Since 1935, technological advances in computers and intellectual advances in mathematical statistics have combined to make the testing of hypotheses in economics less labor intensive and the results more credible. Predictably, economists have responded to this major shift in relative cost-benefit ratios, with the observed modern preoccupation on regression routines. This shift, alone, tends to corroborate Ayres' hypothesis that technology itself independently affects social process. Could the modern emphasis on empirical tests have emerged at all save for computer availability in each research setting?

The larger question, however, concerns the relevance or importance of this development for economics, as a discipline, and the possible distortions in understanding that may have been produced as a result. The opportunity costs of securing proficiency in econometrics are naiveté in basic economic theory itself, naiveté that is manifested in failures to recognize the necessary limits or qualifications with which the elementary propositions of the theory must be hedged. The practical effect is that such limits are ignored with the result that *homo economicus* has come to occupy a more central role than it ever assumed in its putative neoclassical heyday. The basic set of hypotheses tested in modern regressions is derived directly from the assumption that men behave in behalf of narrowly defined and objectively measurable self-interest. There are few, if any, alternative behavioral models behind modern empirical work, although there exist, of course, essentially behavioristic models without any analytical basis. Suppose, for example, that we organize an experiment by placing coins (nickels or dimes) on a sidewalk in a busy central city, and that we observe passersby with a view toward predicting pickup rates. The experiment is conducted and, let us suppose, the initial hypothesis of rational economic behavior is falsified. Men do not, as observed, respond to measured self-interest. But these results may also be "explained" by the fact that other motivations, such as time and trouble or "transactions costs," may have outweighed the measured pecuniary returns. This being the case, however, what will the experimental results have shown? That *homo economicus* does not exist? That economic theory is tautological?

The elementary fact is, of course, that *homo economicus* does exist in the human psyche, along with many other men, and that behavior is a product of the continuing internal struggle among these. The task of economic theory is not that of predicting specific patterns of behavior; it is that of providing a structural understanding of the processes within which the divergent behavioral plans of persons are integrated and reconciled. Knowledge of the strength of the definable economic motivation may be important for making comparisons among institutional-organizational alternatives. But economic theory does not relinquish its explanatory role if its central predictive hypotheses fail to be empirically corroborated. *Homo economicus* need not reign supreme over other men, and his failure to do so does not signal his nonexistence. From this there emerges an implicit organizational norm. When alternatives are possible, social efficiency will be gained by channeling man's self-interest toward mutually compatible goals. This principle, the heart of eighteenth-century wisdom, remains untouched by modern empirical testing, yet the failure of modern economists is measured by their failure at understanding this precept.

This does not suggest that economists should desert their econometric playthings and become modern apologists for market capitalism, as Ayres seemed to classify neoclassical

economic theorists. Nor does it suggest the more likely opposite, that they become the intellectual vanguard for further socialist experimentation. As Knight often remarked,
economists should adopt the morals of the physical scientists even if they should shun the latter's methods. This
morality must include a willingness to go beyond the limits
of empiricism. In effect, modern economists opt out of their
essential moral responsibility by their self-imposed limitation to data-determined inquiries. Ayres' strictures against
the neoclassical purists of the 1920s and 1930s should be as
nothing when compared with those which might be posed
against the sterilities of the econometricians of the 1970s.
The hard questions are not readily formulated in terms of
testable hypothesis. But this offers no cause for not thinking about such questions, for not discussing them, for not
searching for an appreciation and understanding. Empirical
science provides solutions to problems posed, solutions
which, once obtained, become "truth," to be followed by
the invention of new problems and new solutions. "Moral
science" (if I may be permitted to use an old-fashioned
term in what seems to be its proper meaning) is concerned
with age-old "problems," for which "solutions" are, almost
by definition, inappropriate. We do not "solve" the "problem" of social order by producing a unique "solution," regardless of the sophistication of empirical techniques. There
is no objective "truth" to be established here. The "problem"
of social order is faced eternally by men who realize that
they must live together and that to do so they must impose
upon themselves social rules, social institutions. Economics
and economists cannot evade their responsibility in the continuing discourse over such rules and institutions by shifting
attention to trivialities. To the extent that they do so, their

functional roles can only be filled by the charlatans and the fools, whose presence about us requires no demonstration.

Market and Governmental Failure

As noted, Ayres viewed the neoclassical economists of his time as imposing a conceptual model upon economic reality that was, first of all, fallacious, and, second, designed and used deliberately to provide an intellectual-moral defense of a particular form of social order, market capitalism or free enterprise. Viewed in modern perspective, Ayres was somewhat out of date, even in 1935, because the central body of neoclassical theory had already been turned on its head by Pigou, whose great influence seems now to be only remotely correlated with his ability. Ayres should have been ambivalent about the post-Pigovian developments in theoretical welfare economics. Insofar as his strictures were laid against the imposition of a behavioral model which he held to be overly restrictive, Ayres could only have been upset by the theories of market failure that emerged from the marginal-social-product/marginal-private-product calculus of Pigou because this calculus embodied even more restrictive assumptions about human behavior than those which informed the neoclassical models of competitive order. On the other hand, because this theoretical welfare economics did produce market *failure* results, and as such did much to undermine the neoclassical defense of market organization, Ayres might have independently welcomed such developments. In this aspect of the debate, Knight seems clearly to have been corroborated by intellectual developments within economics itself. In a formal sense, pure economic theory is surely value-neutral. The uses to which this theory is put need not be so, and the resort by modern economists to theories of market failure as a means of providing a putative intellectual-moral basis for socialist experimentation is fully comparable to the behavior of the laissez-faire proponents of earlier epochs.

Developments in the 1950s and 1960s, however, offered something of an Hegelian antithesis. *Homo economicus* was introduced to assist in explaining man's behavior in decision roles outside and beyond market exchange, including political or public-choice decisions. Once this simple step was taken, the theorems of governmental or political failure emerged, at least on all fours with the market-failure theorems of post-Pigovian welfare economics. The synthesis, as and when it emerges, can only be represented in a value-free and strictly pragmatic stance. Economic theory can tell us little or nothing about alternative organizational forms, except on a case-by-case basis. Frank Knight would have welcomed some methodological consensus on this point. We cannot be so sure about Clarence Ayres, although some of his students have indeed expressed approval of the "modern institutionalism" that is descriptive of the work of an increasing number of scholars.

The Limits of Self-Interest

Markets fail; governments fail. Demonstration of these propositions is straightforward once *homo economicus* is plugged into the model of interaction. Even in those aspects of economic intercourse that involve no externalities or spillover effects in the Pigovian sense, some limits must be imposed on the working of pure self-interest. Individuals must abide by behavioral standards which dictate adherence to law, respect for property and personal rights, fulfillment of contractual agreements, standards which may not, in specific instances, be consistent with objectively measurable economic self-interest. Absent such standards as these, markets will fail even when there are no imperfections of the sort that have attracted the attention of the welfare theorists. And, of course, even when such standards prevail, markets fail once any of these more familiar imperfections are introduced, failure here being measured against the conceptual ideal. But political attempts at correcting market breakdown also founder on the rocks of measurable economic self-interest of the participants. No person is motivated to undertake the costs of organization that may be required to generate the "public good" that corrective reform represents. Elected and appointed politicians and bureaucrats are not different from other men. They are motivated at least in part by their own interest, not by some higher version of the "social good."

"Social order" requires general acceptance of a minimal set of moral standards. Well-defined laws of property and freedom of market exchange minimize the necessary scope and extension of such standards, but they by no means eliminate them. As individual property rights become confused, and as markets are replaced or subverted by governmental interventions, the dependence of order on some extended range of moral responsibility increases. (So long as the individual confronts market *alternatives,* his dependence on the behavioral pattern of any single person of administrative unit is correspondingly reduced. If he confronts a single governmental or political alternative, his well-being is of necessity put at the mercy of the behavior of a single person or decision unit. In the limit, his dependence is complete.)

Markets do not, however, carry moral weight comparable with their organizational alternatives. Then and now, critics become disturbed at the inequalities that result even from the idealized workings of market processes. These objections, made by Clarence Ayres and by many other old and new critics, do not really concern the division of the gains-from-trade generated by exchange, the realizable surplus that only markets make possible. At base, the objections are to the basic assignment of property rights among persons and families, the allocation of potential "tradeables" among persons *before* they enter market activity. But, and somewhat surprisingly, market institutions themselves are held responsible for their failure to redress these initial imbalances among unequals. Markets are condemned for their failure to produce distributive justice, even if the injustice observed arises in premarket distribution rather than in any sharing of the gains. Comparable failure of the political apparatus to accomplish similar objectives seems not to mitigate the continuing force of this morally based criticism of market order.

Maintenance of a viable social order characterized by substantial individual liberty depends critically on the widespread acceptance of a common set of moral precepts. Such acceptance is by no means assured in our world of the 1970s. These precepts include respect for individual rights, once these are defined in law and/or customary standards of behavior, along with the recognition that the historically determined assignment or allocation of rights among persons may embody significant departures from assignments or allocations that might plausibly emerge from a "renegotiated social contract."[4] This recognition, in turn, should suggest that adjustments may be needed in the structure of rights as such, rather than interferences in the social process through which assigned rights and titles are exchanged among persons. Moral energies should be diverted away from criticisms of markets as such, and distributionally motivated, politically implemented attempts at redress of pre-market injustices shunned. Distributional objectives should be furthered through instruments that operate directly on the underlying extra-market assignment of individuals' rights.

Historical evidence offers little grounds for optimism that the moral energies will be channeled as suggested. Market organization, which minimizes the dependence of man on the morality of his fellows, may continue to be subverted in the mistaken hope that inequalities can be erased. In the attempt, the realizable surplus made available to society only through the working of markets may be dissipated, and the grosser because less tractable inequalities of political power increased.

Institutions, Technology, and Moral Values

Clarence Ayres might not have accepted these conclusions, but the insistence of Ayres and his institutionalist compatriots on the independent importance of institutions and of technology becomes germane to any current examina-

---

[4] For a further discussion of this point, see my paper, "Before Public Choice," in *Explorations in the Theory of Anarchy*, ed. Gordon Tullock (Blacksburg, Va.: Center for Study of Public Choice, 1973); also my book, *The Limits of Liberty: Between Anarchy and Leviathan* (Chicago: University of Chicago Press, 1975).

tion of the moral requirements for social order. Institutions and technology affect the behavior of men, including their acceptance of ethical-moral precepts. Major changes have occurred in the forty years since Ayres and Knight addressed these issues. The institutions of order, the family, the church, and the state, have undergone dramatic change, and the directions of effect on individual adherence to traditional moral standards seem clear.

The family's role in transmitting moral values, including a sense of respect and honor for the institution itself, has been undermined by the shift from the extended unit to the nuclear cell. Ayres might have intervened at this point to add, appropriately, that this changing role for the family is itself traceable to the dramatic changes in technology which moved us off the farms and into the great conurbations. Can urbanized man be expected to live by the moral precepts ideally characteristic of the sturdy yeoman farmer?

The decline of the church as an institution of order, and of orthodox religion as a shaper of the attitudes of men, has perhaps a more tenuous relationship with technology. But this decline is fact, and one that must be reckoned with in any attempt to assess moral requirements. "God Will Take Care of You"—this hymnal statement was meaningful to many more men in 1935 than in the 1970s. Orthodox religion has, by now, almost abandoned its role in softening man's urge to moral wrath against the social structure in which he finds himself. If anything, the modern church has become itself subversive of existing and traditional moral standards, changing its color from an institution of order to one promotive of disorder and instability.

There has been an accompanying change in man's vision of "the state," the governmental-political process. In 1935, man did not know about the Stalinist purges; Hitler was only part way along toward his final solution; the postwar failures in socialist democracies were in the future; the debacles of Great Society programs, the weirdness of the Warren Court and of Watergate were more distant still. Despite the Great Depression, the men of 1935 honored politics and politicians, and patriotism remained extant as a major motive force. There was widespread respect for "law" as such, and rare indeed were those who felt themselves morally capable of choosing individually determined norms for obedience.

Alongside these disintegrating institutions, which tended to establish and to maintain order and stability in society, with the predictable effects of such disintegration on individual adherence to traditional moral norms, the school must be placed. Within the context of strong and stable institutions of family, church, and state, the school can appropriately combine a rational transmission of moral values with a critical and searching reexamination of these values. As the offsets are weakened, however, and as the internal mix within the school changes toward criticism and away from transmitting value, this institution becomes one of disorder and instability in modern society.

The institutional developments alone, independent of technology, would have placed increasing pressure on the sometimes fragile stability of social order. This pressure has been enhanced by technological change, which has exerted independent influence. The genuine revolution that has occurred in transportation and communication has helped to create a highly mobile society, with the result that "locational loyalty," as a force making for moral value stability, has largely disappeared. Perhaps even more important, what has been, and what will be, the impact of television on individual attitudes and behavior in all sorts of social interaction, in the marketplace, in the voting booth, in the day-to-day adherence to ordinary standards of conduct, in manners? Will mass television so modify behavior patterns as to make adjustments in the institutional constraints, in legal order, necessary, or if not necessary, desired? Can the basic norms of a free society be extended to cover this medium? Is "freedom of the press" automatically extendable here, or do we require a new definition?

Conclusion

These are not "economic" questions as such, so few modern economists bother to ask them, much less attempt to provide answers. And to their shame, for it is precisely these issues and these questions that would have occupied the minds of both Clarence Ayres and Frank Knight in the 1970s. These two would have, no doubt, continued to disagree sharply on both diagnosis and prescription, but at the same time both would have treated the piddling trivialities that occupy modern economists with the contempt that they deserve.

Retrospectively, we might say that both Ayres and Knight should have been admonished in 1935 by the Adam Smith statement: "There's a deal of ruin in a nation." Forty years later we live in a more affluent but still tolerably free society that has not suffered moral collapse. The optimistic critic would be tempted to apply much the same admonition to my own assessment. Despite the institutional and technological changes that have occurred, there may be major elements of stability in our society that I have tended to overlook in my discussion. Perhaps the excesses of the 1960s were aberrations from the more orderly development of a social order embodying affluence, justice, and freedom. Perhaps. But hoping will not make things so, and those of us who do sense the vulnerability of social order to what seem to us to be gradual but unmistakable changes in the moral bases of this order would be derelict in our own duty if we did not raise warning flags.

12

Markets, States, and the Extent of Morals

M an acts within a set of institutional constraints that have developed historically: in part by sheer accident; in part by survival in a social evolutionary process; in part by technological necessity; in part by constructive design (correctly or incorrectly conceived). These constraints which define the setting within which human behavior must take place may, however, be inconsistent with man's capacities as a genuine "social animal." To the extent that moral-ethical capacities are "relatively absolute,"[1] there may be only one feasible means of reducing the impact of the inconsistency. Attempts must be made to modify the *institutions* (legal, political, social, economic) with the objective of matching these more closely with the empirical realities of man's moral limitations.

In a certain restricted sense, the observed behavior of the modern American is excessively "self-interested." Rather

This chapter is reprinted from *American Economic Review* 68 (May 1978): 364–68. Permission to reprint is herewith acknowledged. I am indebted to Roger Congleton, Thomas Ireland, Janet Landa, Robert Tollison, and Richard Wagner for helpful suggestions.

[1] Reinhold Niebuhr, *Moral Man and Immoral Society* (New York, 1932), pp. 3, 267.

than hope for a "new morality," I shall focus on the potential for institutional reform that may indirectly modify man's behavior toward his fellows. Institutions may have been allowed to develop and to persevere that exacerbate rather than mitigate man's ever-present temptation to act as if he were an island, with others treated as part of his natural environment. In a properly qualified sense, the latter pattern of behavior is the economist's "ideal," but the costs have not been adequately recognized.

Let me proceed by simple illustration. Consider two traders, each of whom is initially endowed with a commodity bundle. Gains from trade exist and cooperation through trade is suggested, but there arises the complementary conflict over the sharing of net surplus. As we extend the model by introducing additional traders, however, the conflict element of the interaction is squeezed out, and, in the limit, each trader becomes a pure price-taker. "In perfect competition there is no competition," as Frank Knight was fond of emphasizing. (However, we must never lose sight of the elementary fact that this "economic ideal," including its most complex variants, presumes the existence of laws and institutions that secure private property and enforce contracts.)

Let me change the illustration and now assume that the same two persons find themselves in a genuine "publicness" interaction. (They are villagers alongside the swamp, to use David Hume's familiar example.) As before, there exist potential gains from trade, and these can be secured by agreement. Cooperation and conflict again enter to influence choice behavior, but here the introduction of more traders does nothing to squeeze down the range of conflict.

Indeed, it does quite the opposite. Beyond some critical limit, each person will come to treat the behavior of others as part of the state of nature that he confronts as something wholly independent of his own actions.

Numbers work in opposite directions in the two cases. Under a set of laws and institutions that are restricted to the security of property and contract, the extension of the market in partitionable goods moves the efficiency frontier of the community outward. But, under the same laws and institutions, if there exist nonpartitionable interdependencies (public goods), an increase in the size of the group may move the attainable efficiency frontier inward.

I have introduced the familiar private-goods/public-goods comparison to illustrate my general argument to the effect that there are opposing behavioral implications involved in any extension in the membership of a community. The effects of group size on choice behavior, and through this on the normative evaluation of institutions, have not been sufficiently explored by economists, most of whom have remained content to concentrate on the formal efficiency properties of allocations. With relatively few exceptions they have worked with fixed-size groups. And even in 1978, most economic policy discussion proceeds on the implicit presumption that "government" is benevolently despotic.[2]

What is the orthodox economists' response when pure public goods are postulated? It is relatively easy to define the formal conditions that are necessary for allocative effi-

---

[2] Economists have continued for eight decades to ignore the warnings of Knut Wicksell (*Finanztheoretische Untersuchungen* [Jena, 1896]).

ciency, but it is not possible to define the governmental process that might generate these results.[3] Work in public-choice theory has contributed to our understanding of how governmental processes actually operate, but this theory is, in a general sense, one of governmental failure rather than success.

Political scientists have objected to the imperialism of public-choice economists who extend utility-maximizing models of behavior to persons who act variously in collective-choice roles, as voters, as politicians, and as bureaucrats. These critics intuitively sense that a polity driven solely by utility maximizers (with empirical content in the maximand) cannot possibly generate an escape from the large-number analogue to the prisoners' dilemma suggested in the simple example of a public-goods interaction. These critics have not, however, understood the basic causes for the general dilemma that modern collectivist institutions impose on citizens, politicians, and bureaucrats. Even more than the economists, orthodox political scientists have tended to ignore the possible effects of group, or community size on individual behavior patterns.

Any political act is, by definition, "public" in the classic Samuelsonian sense. An act of voting by a citizen potentially affects a result that, once determined, will be applied to *all* members of the community. Similarly, an act by a legislator in voting for one tax rule rather than another becomes an input in determining a result that will define the environment for all members of the polity. Comparable

---

[3] A possible qualification to this statement is required with reference to the demand-revealing process, summarized by T. Nicolaus Tideman and Gordon Tullock ("A New and Superior Process for Making Social Choice," *Journal of Political Economy* 84 [December 1976]: 1145–60).

conclusions extend to each and every act of a civil servant and to each decision of a judge.[4] Under what conditions could we predict that such political acts will provide public good? For instruction here, we can return directly to our elementary example. We should expect at least some such behavior to exhibit cooperative features in effectively small groups. We should not, and could not, expect persons who act politically to provide public goods voluntarily in large-number settings.

We can reach this conclusion by economic analysis that incorporates standard utility-maximizing behavior on the part of all actors. My principal hypothesis, however, involves the possible inconsistency between man's *moral* capacities and the institutions within which he acts. Is not man capable of surmounting the generalized public-goods dilemma of modern politics by moral-ethical principles that will serve to constrain his proclivities toward aggrandizement of his narrowly defined self-interest? It is here that my secondary hypothesis applies. The force of moral-ethical principle in influencing behavior is directly dependent on the size of community within which action takes place. Other things equal, the smaller the number of persons with whom a person interacts, the higher the likelihood that he will seem to behave in accordance with something akin to the Kantian generalization principle: in our terminology, that he will provide public good in his choice behavior.

Even this secondary hypothesis can be discussed in a way as to bring it within a utility-maximizing framework. The extent that a person expects his own behavior to influ-

---

[4] See Gordon Tullock, "Public Decisions as Public Goods," *Journal of Political Economy* 79 (July–August 1971): 913–18.

ence the behavior of those with whom he interacts will depend on the size of the group. Hence, utility maximization in a small-number setting will not exhibit the observable properties of utility maximization in a large-number setting.[5] I want, however, to go beyond this strictly small group phenomenon of direct behavioral feedback. I want to introduce moral ethical constraints in a genuine non-economic context here. I propose to allow *homo economicus* to exist only as one among many men that describe human action, and in many settings to assume a tertiary motivation role.

The precise dimension of human behavior that I concentrate on here is the location of the effective mix between the two motivational forces of economic self-interest and what I shall term "community."[6] I do not want, and I have no need, to identify with any particular variant of non-self-interest: fellowship, brotherhood, Christian love, empathy, Kantian imperative, sympathy, public interest, or anything else. I want only to recognize the existence of a general motive force that inhibits the play of narrowly defined self-interest when an individual recognizes himself to be a member of a group of others more or less like himself. Robinson Crusoe could be motivated by nothing other than self-interest until Friday arrives. Once he acknowledges the existence of Friday, a tension develops and Crusoe finds that his behavior is modified. This tension exists in all human action and observed behavior reflects the outcome of

[5] See my "Ethical Rules, Expected Values, and Large Numbers," *Ethics* 74 (October 1965): 1–13.

[6] In a tautological sense, all behavior, including that which I label moral-ethical, can be analyzed in a utility-maximizing model. In this paper, however, "utility maximization" and "self-interest" are defined operationally.

some solution of the inner conflict. The institutional setting determines the size of community relevant for individual behavior. This influence of size is exerted both directly in the sense of limits to recognition, and indirectly in the relationship between a community's membership and its ability to command personal loyalties. Conceptually, the "structure of community" within which an individual finds himself can shift the location of behavior along a spectrum bounded on one extreme by pure self-interest and on the other by pure community interest within which the actor counts for no more than any other member.

The institutions (economic, geological, legal, political, social, technological), which define the sizes of community within which an individual finds himself, impose *external* bounds on possible behavior. Parallel to these external constraints there are also *internal* limits or bounds on what we may call an individual's moral-ethical community. There are, of course, no sharp categorical lines to be drawn between those other persons whom someone deems "members of the tribe" and those whom he treats as "outsiders." I make no such claim. I assert only that, for any given situation, there is a difference in an individual's behavior toward members and nonmembers, and that the membership lists are drawn up in his own psyche. This is not to say either that persons are uniform with respect to their criteria for tribal membership or that these criteria are invariant with respect to exogenous events. Clearly, neither of these inferences will hold. However, the fact of behavioral discrimination is empirical and subject to test. I am not arguing normatively to the effect that individuals should or should not discriminate among other members of the human species, or even between humans and other animals.

My colleague Tullock enjoys asking egalitarians whether they would extend their precepts for social justice to the people of Bangladesh. He gets few satisfactory answers. Why should precepts for distributive justice mysteriously stop at the precise boundaries of the nation-state? If one responds that they need not do so, that national boundaries are arbitrary products of history, then one is led to ask whether or not effective precepts of justice might stop short of such inclusive community, whether or not the moral-ethical limit for most persons is reached short of the size of modern nations.[7] At provincial or regional boundaries? At the local community level? The extended family? The clan? The racial group? The ethnic heritage? The church membership? The functional group?

What can a person be predicted to do when the external institutions force upon him a role in a community that extends beyond his moral-ethical limits? The tension shifts toward the self-interest pole of behavior; moral-ethical principles are necessarily sublimated. The shift is exaggerated when a person realizes that others in the extended community of arbitrary and basically amoral size will find themselves in positions comparable to his own. How can a person act politically in other than his own narrowly defined self-interest in an arbitrarily sized nation of more than 200 million? Should we be at all surprised when we observe the increasing usage of the arms and agencies of the national government for the securing of private personal gain?

---

[7] In an argument related to that in this paper, Dennis Mueller concentrates on the relationship between the size of community and the ability of a person to imagine himself behind a Rawlsian veil of ignorance ("Achieving the Just Polity," *American Economic Review Proceedings* 64 [May 1974]: 147–52).

The generalized public-goods dilemma of politics can be kept within tolerance limits only if there is some proximate correspondence between the external institutional and the internal moral constraints on behavior.[8] This century may be described by developments that drive these two sets of constraints apart. An increase in population alone reduces the constraining influence of moral rules. Moreover population increase has been accompanied by increasing mobility over space, by the replacement of local by national markets, by the urbanization of society, by the shift of power from state-local to national government, and by the increased politicization of society generally. Add to this the observed erosion of the family, the church, and the law—all of which were stabilizing influences that tended to reinforce moral precepts—and we readily understand why *homo economicus* has assumed such a dominant role in modern behavior patterns.[9]

Indirect evidence for the general shift from morally based resolution of conflict and morally based settlement of terms of cooperation to political-legal instruments is provided by the observed rapidly increasing resort to litigation. Modern man seeks not to live with his neighbor, but to become an island, even when his natural setting dictates moral community. This movement, in its turn, prompts lawyers to turn to economic theory for new normative instruction.

---

[8] Gerald Sirkin refers to the "Victorian compromise," which is, in several respects, similar to the correspondence noted here (see Sirkin, "Resource X and the Theory of Retrodevelopment" in Robert D. Leiter and Stanley J. Friedlander, eds., *The Economics of Resources* [New York, 1976], pp. 193–208).

[9] My diagnosis is restricted to the Western, specifically the American, setting. Perhaps the strongest empirical support for my argument is, however, provided in non-Western collectivized countries through the observed failures to create "new men" via institutional change.

Despite the flags and the tall ships of 1976, there is relatively little moral-ethical cement in the United States which might bring the internal moral-ethical limits more closely in accord with the external community defined inclusively by the national government. There is no "moral equivalent to war," and since Vietnam, we must question whether war itself can serve such a function. Nonetheless, experience suggests that war and the threat thereof may be the only moral force that might sustain the governmental Leviathan. Viewed in this light, it is ominous that each president, soon after entering office, shifts his attention away from the divisive issues of domestic politics toward those of foreign affairs. We must beware the shades of Orwell's *1984*, when external enemies are created, real or imaginary, for the purpose of sustaining domestic moral support for the national government.

While I am not some agrarian utopian calling for a return to the scattered villages on the plains, I shall accept the label of a constitutional utopian who can still see visions of an American social order that would not discredit our Founding Fathers. To achieve such an order, drastic constitutional change is surely required. Effective federalism remains possible, within the technological constraints of the age, and "constitutional revolution" need not require the massive suffering, pestilence, and death associated with revolution on the left or right. Dramatic devolution might succeed in channeling some of the moral-ethical fervor in politics toward constructive rather than destructive purpose.

I become discouraged when I observe so little discussion, even among scholars, of the federal alternative to the enveloping Leviathan. Where is the Quebec of the United States? Where is the Scotland? Could a threat of secession now succeed? More important, could the emergence of such a threat itself force some devolution of central government power? Who will join me in offering to make a small contribution to the Texas Nationalist Party? Or to the Nantucket Separatists? From small beginnings . . .

We should be clear about the alternative. The scenario to be played out in the absence of dramatic constitutional reform involves increasing resort to the power of the national government by those persons and groups who seek private profit and who are responding predictably to the profit opportunities that they observe to be widening. Individually, they cannot be expected to understand that the transfer game is negative sum, and, even with such understanding, they cannot be expected to refrain from investment in rent seeking. Furthermore, as persons and groups initially outside the game come to observe their own losses from political exploitation, they too will enter the lists. As the process moves forward through time, we can predict a continued erosion of trust in politics and politicians. But distrust will not turn things around. "Government failure" against standard efficiency norms may be demonstrated analytically and empirically, but I see no basis for the faith that such demonstrations will magically produce institutional reform. I come back to constitutional revolution as the only attractive alternative to the scenario that we seem bent to act out. In the decade ahead, we shall approach the bicentenary of the Constitution itself. Can this occasion spark the dialogue that must precede action?

13

Equality as
Fact and Norm

$\mathbb{E}$ conomists often introduce the simplifying assumption that all persons are equal or identical in order to make their abstract models of human interaction more tractable. In a world of equals, analysis of the behavioral responses of a single person yields results that are automatically generalizable of the whole community. Models embodying these assumptions may retain explanatory value even when their descriptively unreal nature is fully recognized. The predictive potential is enhanced when the identity assumptions can be restricted to selected characteristics or attributes. Any generalized prediction in social science implies as its basis a theoretical model that embodies elements of an equality assumption. If individuals differ, one from the other, in all attributes, social science becomes impossible. In an ideal sense, the role of the social scientist is limited to explanation and prediction, and it does not extend to the formulation of norms for social organization. Nonetheless, the underlying purpose of scientific explanation must be acknowledged to be improvement. Those who partici-

This chapter is reprinted without substantial change from *Ethics* 81 (April 1971): 228–40. Permission to reprint is herewith acknowledged.

pate in social and institutional reform (including social scientists in other roles than scientific) act on the basis of some vision of social process. This vision is shaped by the scientists' explanatory models.

In this chapter I shall argue that the continuing debate between the individualist and the collectivist may be grounded on divergent visions of social process and not necessarily or fundamentally on differing ultimate values. Further, I shall demonstrate how the basic difference may reduce to one involving the implicit assumptions made about personal differences. The individualist and the collectivist select different attributes of equality to be dominant characteristics in their model visions of social interaction. To the extent that this hypothesis holds, the issue between the two political philosophies may be primarily empirical. Saying this is not to imply that the issue is amenable to straightforward resolution. If, however, agreement could be reached on the sources of disagreement, prospects for constructive dialogue might be enhanced.

The discussion is intended to be general, but it has direct relevance to the current social scene. The social discontent in evidence in East and West can be interpreted as providing empirical refutation, even if indirectly, of one variant of the equality assumption. Individuals seem to be rejecting the implied equality of collectivism. Whether or not this rejection is, or may be, coupled with an increased acceptance of the implied equality of individualism remains an open question.

The Attributes of Equality

Economists state their assumptions somewhat more carefully than their fellow social scientists, and it will be helpful to commence with the economists' specifications for a world of equals. Normally, they discuss two separate attributes of identity or equality among individuals. One of these relates to the demand or consumption side of personal behavior and the other relates to the supply or producing side. For the demand or consumption side, these are summarized in the interchangeable terms: *preferences, tastes, utility functions.* For the supply or producing side, these are summarized in the terms: *factor* or *resource endowments, capacities, production-transformation possibilities.* In a full world-of-equals model, persons are postulated to be identical in both attributes, in preferences and in factor endowments or capacities. For some purposes, economists find it useful to retain the identity assumption on the utility-function or preferences side while dropping the corollary assumption on the capacities side. For example, an equal-preferences model has proven helpful in "explaining" some of the widely observed fiscal institutions in modern societies. For other purposes, the economist finds it helpful to drop the assumption of equal preferences while retaining that about equal capacities. This is essentially the model employed for explaining those interoccupational wage or salary differentials that are "equalizing."

My reference here to economists' frequent use of models that embody assumptions about individual equality should not be interpreted as suggesting that such restrictions are necessary in the central models of economic theory. For the most part, this theory is developed in a context of inequality among persons, both with respect to utility functions and to resource endowments. As economic theory assists in informing an overall or comprehensive vision of the socio-economic interaction process, however, the relative patterns of inequality that are assumed to be present in the two attributes may well exercise significant influence. While acknowledging interpersonal inequalities in both preferences and capacities, the normative implications of specific institutional-organization structures may depend critically on the relative degree of inequality imputed to each attribute. Roughly similar results may be predicted with theoretical models that implicitly embody widely differing assumptions, and existing empirical techniques remain far from that level of sophistication that would be required for definitive testing.

Equality in Preferences and in Capacities

Initially I shall discuss the all-market and the all-collective organizational alternatives under a pure world-of-equals assumption. All persons are assumed to be identical, both in preferences and in capacities. Identity in preferences means that all persons classify "goods" and "bads" in the same way, and, furthermore, that they make the same subjective trade-offs among the separate arguments in these two sets. In formal economic theory, the arguments in the utility functions of individuals are normally limited to "economic" goods and bads. For our purposes, equality in preferences or tastes should be extended to encompass "noneconomic" arguments. Identity in preferences implies not only that all persons place the same relative evaluation on apples, oranges, and smog, but also that they place the same relative evaluation on reduced military posture in the Far East and increased military posture in the Middle East.

A rigorous definition of identity in capacities or endowments is less familiar and considerably more complex. In a static context, identity among persons in endowments means that each one confronts the same production-transformation prospects. Each person commences with the same set of goods and bads, and he faces the same prospects of "trading" these one with another. This static definition is overly restrictive, however, because of the intertemporal interdependence of individual choices about the utilization of capacities. By choosing to use his initial endowment in one way rather than another at one point in time, a person can permanently increase or decrease his endowment or capacity. Any reasonable definition of identity in endowments or in capacities must, therefore, specify that persons face the same production-transformation possibilities at some designated point in time, normally before the start of the income-earning period, which would presumably be at some moment of career or occupational choice. Only with some such definition as this can the capacity-equality assumption have much relevance independent from the preferences assumption. Defined in this way, individuals may actually differ in resource capabilities, human and nonhuman, at any one point in time even though the model postulates strict identity. The actual differences at any time must be attainable by the exercise of individual choice dating from the initial point at which capacities were in fact identical. We should note that this definitional complexity does not arise in the pure world-of-equals model. When we postulate identity in utility functions, this implies that all persons will choose to use their capacities identically and hence will remain identical through time. However, when we drop this assumption of identity in preferences in later discussion, the definitional extension of the equal-capacity assumption becomes essential.

In the pure world of equals, embodying both identity among all persons in preferences and identity among all persons in capacities, similar results are generated under widely differing institutional-organizational arrangements. Hence, the "constitutional" choice among separate social structures is not an important consideration. To demonstrate this, we may compare and contrast collectivist and noncollectivist or individualistic organization of an economy under the extreme equality assumption.

Let us assume that the production of all goods and services is organized through a market process in which all persons remain free to make whatever producing-trading-consuming decisions they desire. If we assume only that contracts are enforced and that fraud is effectively policed, this economy will be characterized by substantial identity in final consumption patterns among all individuals.[1]

Let us compare this result with that which might be predicted to emerge under a dramatically different organizational structure. We assume now that the economy is fully collectivized. All decisions are made through a collective or political choice process. If we assume only that arbitrary exploitation or personal discrimination is effectively pre-

---

[1] In an extreme variant of this model, which embodies constant returns to scale of production over all ranges of output for all goods, all of which are private, this economy would be without trade. In such a setting, each person becomes a complete microcosm of the whole society. In the less restricted setting where constant returns are not assumed, individuals will be led to specialize in production and differentials in wages and salaries will emerge that will offset the relative advantages of the several occupations. To the extent that such differentials in income emerge, individuals can differ, one from another, in command over final product, and full identity in consumption patterns will be violated. Such differentials are required, however, to keep persons on the same utility levels. If we assume away the differences in the subjective advantages of differing occupations, this complexity will not arise.

vented, this structure, regardless of the particular decision rule that is adopted, will generate results that are quite similar to those that characterize the all-market economy. This similarity in results between these wholly different organizational alternatives may appear surprising. It stems basically from the identity assumption under the restrictions imposed on each decision process.

In the all-collective economy, the effective prevention of arbitrary discrimination requires that each person be treated in the same manner as his equals, which in this case means that all persons are treated identically regardless of the collective decisions that are made. This applies for the cost as well as for the benefit side. This means that no person can, through his membership in a dominant political coalition, secure gains at the expense of his equals outside the coalition. Every decision rule produces results that are the same as those that would emerge under a rule that requires unanimous consent. An example may be helpful here. Suppose that one man is appointed as dictator; he is authorized to make all decisions in the community. He will, of course, choose among alternatives on the basis of his own preferences, but since his preferences are identical with those of everyone else, he will make the same choices that everyone else will desire that he make. He could secure differential personal gains from his dictatorship position only if he should somehow discriminate between his own position and those of his fellow equals. Under genuine nondiscriminatory collectivism, this is not possible. All decision rules generate, therefore, the same results.[2]

The no-discrimination requirement for the all-collective

---

[2] For a further discussion of this proposition, see my *Demand and Supply of Public Goods* (Chicago: Rand McNally, 1968), pp. 164–66.

economy serves the same purpose as the no-fraud requirement for the all-market economy. If fraud becomes possible
in market dealings among persons, even among those who
are initially assumed to be equal, some must assume the
role of the defrauders and some must become the victims
of fraud. The differential ability to defraud along with the
differential ability to secure personal gains through political
or collective discrimination violates the basic equality assumption. This assumption is critical for the comparative
purposes that this analysis embodies.

With the nondiscriminatory qualifications, the all-collective economy will generate an equality among all persons
in final consumption patterns just as will the all-market
economy. Collective agreement on this pattern will be
reached readily and, significantly, all persons will acquiesce
in the chosen results since they will mirror their own preferences regardless of the decision rule. The important conclusion for our purposes is that the all-collective economy and
the all-market economy produce roughly the same results.
These sharply divergent institutional-organizational alternatives generate significant differences in results only to the
extent that men differ one from another.

Differential Preferences and Equal Capacities

The question becomes: How do men differ, and how will
differences over particular attributes modify these comparative results? The dichotomy of attributes is helpful. We
shall first compare the organizational alternatives in a model
that embodies the assumption that all persons remain identical in capacities, as earlier defined, but where they are
allowed to differ in preferences. Individual utility functions

are no longer the same. In one sense, and as the analysis will reveal, this is the economist's standard model. In many economic applications, "the individual" is described by his preference scale or his utility function.

Let us consider, as before, an all-market structure qualified only by the enforcement of contracts and the policing of fraud. Since individuals now have different tastes their final consumption patterns will not be uniform. Trade will be observed to take place until each person commands that set of consumption goods and services which most nearly satisfies his own unique trade-offs. The assumption that persons remain equal in capacity ensures that the differences among final consumption bundles stem almost exclusively from the postulated differences in preferences.[3] For reasons noted earlier, individuals at any time may face different production-transformation possibilities even in this equal-capacities model. To the extent that they do so, real incomes, and hence command over final product, may differ. But such differences as these arise themselves from the individuals' own decisions made earlier about increasing or running down initially held endowments.

The differences in final consumption bundles that would be observed in the all-market economy in this model cannot be interpreted as having been imposed by forces external to the individuals. These differences reflect the inherent individualities of the persons that are involved and nothing more. In such a context, it seems evident that "greater equality" carries little meaning and that it could hardly be advanced seriously as a norm for social change.

---

[3] The "almost" is inserted to allow for the differentials discussed in footnote 1.

Let us now change the postulated organizational structure while remaining within the differential-preferences/equal-capacities model. Assume that an all-collective constitution is in being. All decisions concerning the allocation and the utilization of resources are made in a collective or political process. As before, we also postulate that there is an effective restriction against arbitrary discrimination among persons or groups. In this setting, individuals would tend to be provided with uniform patterns of final consumption, despite their differences in tastes. The central characteristic of nondiscriminatory collectivism is universality or uniformity in treatment.[4] The particular characteristics of the consumption bundle that will be provided uniformly for all persons will depend on the rule through which collective decisions are made. When the collective decision rule is that of simple majority voting, the person or persons whose preferences are median for the whole community will tend to be controlling. Under other decision rules, the preferences of the median member of the effective electorate will dominate the outcomes. Under single-person dictatorship this reduces, of course, to his own preferences. The outcome depends on the rules for making group choice and, in any case, individualized expressions of preference or taste could

---

[4] Somewhat surprisingly, the implications of this uniformity-universality characteristic of nondiscriminatory collectivism were not fully discussed in the traditional economic analysis of socialist organization. Several recent papers have been aimed at filling this gap. See Gordon Tullock, "Social Cost and Governmental Action," *American Economic Review* 59 (May 1969): 189–97; Yorum Barzel, "Two Propositions on the Optimum Level of Producing Collective Goods," *Public Choice* 6 (Spring 1969): 31–38; C. M. Lindsay, "Medical Care and the Economics of Sharing," *Economica* 36 (November 1969): 351–69; along with my own, "Notes for an Economic Theory of Socialism," *Public Choice* 8 (Spring 1970): 29–44.

not be predicted to emerge under any rule. In the final solution, large numbers of persons must remain dissatisfied by the common standards of consumption that are imposed. The uniformity in consumption bundles is achieved only through the repression of individual differences in tastes.

As this organizational scheme would actually work, individuals would have strong incentives to retrade goods and services among themselves after some initial collective or governmental distribution. To the extent that such retrading takes place, individualized tastes could be expressed. If this sort of trading were allowed, however, we should be outside the range of our all-collective model. For comparative purposes, it seems best to restrict analysis to a pure collective model, in which all such retrading as this would be prohibited.

As the description of this differential-preferences/equal-capacities model should make clear, it provides the strongest case for adopting the market process as the organizational norm. The imposed equalities in final consumption patterns that collectivism produces take on no normative features. For those who place strong positive value on individual freedom of expression, on individual and personal liberty, in their conception of the "good society," the market offers major advantages over its collectivist counterpart. It allows individuals to express their separate preferences while these are necessarily stifled, to greater or lesser degree, under wholesale collectivization of activity. Conversely, for those who may value individual freedom somewhat less intensely and who place relatively more weight on distributional equality, the collectivist alternative offers relatively little advantage here. The distributional inequalities in final consumption that characterize the market results in this framework do not arise from differences in initial endowments. "Distributive justice" simply cannot be invoked in ethical support of a collectively imposed set of uniformities in consumption. Insofar as the equalities in capacities, the assumption of this model, are equalities in fact, equality in consumption cannot be introduced as a norm.

Only one minor qualification need be added. To make these conclusions generally acceptable, we should include in individual capacities the ability to "be lucky." If there are significant uncertainties present, individuals with equal initial endowments may find their final consumption possibilities determined, in part, by sheer luck. An argument may be advanced in support of equalization to correct partially for such fortuitous differentials. Realistically, of course, comparable or even greater uncertainty would be present under the collectivist alternative.

Identical Preferences and Differential Capacities

We may proceed predictably in our analysis by reversing the assumptions about equality. We now assume that all persons in the community are identical in tastes or preferences but that they differ in capacities or endowments, human and unhuman. We shall examine the results to be predicted under the contrasting institutional structures.

In an effectively working market process, individuals would be observed to consume different final consumption bundles despite the initially postulated identity in utility functions. The position that a particular person attains on his utility surface will depend on his resource or factor endowments (including luck) and this model postulates that these endowments differ as among separate persons. The market continues to allow for a full expression of individualized preferences, but these are restricted by the initial differentials in capacities.

These results may be compared with those predicted to emerge under the all-collective structure. As previously emphasized, there will be a tendency here for individuals to be provided with uniform consumption bundles. Interestingly, if all persons should find themselves in this model with identical sets of "goods," there would be no overt dissatisfaction at this stage. Even if all prohibitions on retrading were eliminated here, none would be observed to take place. The reason is, of course, the postulated equality in tastes among all persons in the group. In the final equilibrium produced by the all-collective structure, which would be characterized by consumption uniformity, individuals would not be directly coerced into an acceptance of a final-goods package contrary to their own preferences.

This suggests that the results of the all-collective structure or process under this model's set of assumptions would be more stable in some political-sociological sense than those emerging in the earlier model. This is correct, but an important consideration that has been so far neglected must now be explicitly discussed. The decision-making process in the all-collective structure under equal preference and differential capacities must be examined closely. In one sense what is required here is a more careful specification of the differential-capacities assumption in this setting. In the earlier definition, we limited capacity to production-transformation prospects that faced the individual, production-transformation prospects for producing-exchanging "economic" goods and services. We said nothing about the capacities of persons in the political process. In one respect, we have assumed throughout our analysis that all persons possess equal capacities to influence collectively determined outcomes. This "political equality" assumption is the basis for the postulated uniformity in consumption under collective organization. If differences among persons in capacities to produce economic values are accompanied by differences in capacities to produce values through the political process, the market and the collective-decision structure would tend to generate roughly the same results in all cases. In the model under consideration in this section, we want to retain the assumption about equality in "political capacity" but allow for differential capacities to produce economic values. If we then impose uniformity in consumption as a result of collective decision-making, we must require that individuals, with different economic capacities, make differing contributions to costs. Obviously, if capacities to produce goods and services differ among persons, and if these capacities are to be fully utilized, the equalization of final consumption bundles among all persons must involve differential shares in the costs of producing those goods that are produced.

Understanding may be facilitated here if we compare this all-collective result with that result discussed earlier under the differential-preference/equal-capacities model. In the latter, individuals would presumably be subjected to non-discriminatory "tax payments," and because capacities are identical, these are roughly the same for each person. Individuals are unhappy or dissatisfied with the all-collective structure because of the imposed uniformities in consumption bundles in the face of differing tastes. By contrast, under the model treated in this section, individuals acquiesce in the consumption bundles that are uniformly imposed under all-collective decision-making because their utility functions are the same. Those whose capacities are superior may remain unhappy in the fact that their own imposed contribution to total production exceeds those made by others. But since capacities or endowments cannot be directly exchanged, there is no available means for redress.[5] The same thing can be put in the language of theoretical welfare economics or of game theory. The all-collective results in the equal-preferences/differential-capacities model treated in this section need not be, but conceptually could be, Pareto optimal. Hence, in such case any proposals for change would become analogous to plays in a zero-sum game. By contrast, the all-collective results in the differential-preferences/equal-capacities model treated earlier must be nonoptimal. Proposals to modify these results can conceptually secure unanimous consent of all parties; the game is positive sum.

It should be clear from the discussion that the collectivist has an immensely stronger argument in this equal-preferences/differential-capacities model than he does in its converse, examined earlier. The costs of enforcing collectively chosen outcomes are lower, which is the same as saying that these outcomes are more stable. Relative to the situation predictable in the converse setting, the collectivist also stands on firmer economic ground here. He cannot, of course, carry the day even here on pure efficiency criteria, but the possible inefficiencies of collectivism are relatively less significant.

The individualist's arguments are relatively less potent

---

[5] This statement would have to be qualified to the extent that persons have locational alternatives available to them. If persons can migrate to other communities, if they can "vote with their feet," indirect trade can take place.

here. Insofar as individual preferences are, in fact, identical, his argument for allowing differential expressions of these is undermined. His support of market process that stems normatively from the supposition that "men are different" rests solely on the initial differences in capacities or endowments. The end objectives, the "goods" that men seek, are identical for all men. Their differences in final attainment under unfettered market interaction stem almost exclusively from differences in the means with which they are provided. It is here that "distributive justice" takes on significant ethical properties. The individualist who defends market organization will rarely argue for inequalities in final consumption bundles that arise solely from capacity differences. His defense of the market here must rest largely, if not exclusively, on efficiency grounds; he must advance quite different arguments from those that seem effective in the equal-capacities model.

The World of Unequals

It is, of course, recognized that individuals differ, one from the other, in both of the essential attributes discussed. Men are unequal in preferences; they do not possess identical utility functions. Men also differ in capacities; even at some defined point in time, inequality in endowments (human and nonhuman) is characteristic of the real world. It is also evident that no social reformer proposes either an all-market or an all-collective institutional arrangement. The continuing debate between the collectivist and the individualist concerns the appropriate dividing line between market and collective order, always within a structure that includes both a private and a public or governmental sector.

Analytically, however, the extreme models about personal equality and about institutional structure are suggestive. They may indicate some of the implicit empirical biases of those who stand on opposing sides of the arguments about social reform. The individualist who seeks to shift the organizational spectrum toward the market pole, who seeks to decollectivize activities currently in the public sector, may interpret and explain the inequalities that he observes on the basis of differences among persons in preferences, including preferences about capacity utilization (for example, choices for work versus leisure, spending versus saving, etc.), at least to a relatively greater extent than his collectivist counterpart.[6] To the extent that he acknowledges capacity-generated inequalities in distribution, the individualist is likely to propose reforms that are aimed at equalizing initial endowments or at least mitigating extreme inequalities. He seeks reform and social changes that have as their objective the achievement of some plausibly satisfactory approximation to the differential-preferences/equal-capacities model. In contraposition, the collectivist, who seeks to shift the organizational spectrum in the opposing direction, who seeks to remove still more activities from the market process and to collectivize them, may interpret and explain the inequalities that he observes (the same reality confronted by the individualist) on the basis of individual differences in inherent capacities, at least

---

[6] An alternative hypothesis would allow the individualist to attribute observed inequalities among persons to the same sources as does his collectivist counterpart but to be more pessimistic about the possibilities of removing such inequalities through collective action. The whole set of problems raised by the prospects of effectively controlling bureaucratic hierarchies cannot be neglected, but these are not central to the main theme of this chapter.

to some relatively greater extent than does the individualist. If he could conceive of equalized capacities, the collectivist would probably predict the emergence of what he might regard as only trivial differences in final consumption patterns, differences that he might attribute to whim and fashion rather than to genuine tastes or values. In his vision of the world, individuals really do want the same things; the inequalities that are observed must, therefore, reflect capacity differentials. As he comes to propose reforms, the collectivist may pay relatively little attention to capacity equalization, per se. He may regard attempts to make individuals equal in initial endowments, attempts to "equalize opportunities," as both indirect and inefficient means to secure distributive justice. In his vision, even the most massive of such attempts may produce limited results. He agrees with Plato and disagrees with Adam Smith about the differences between the common street porter and the philosopher. Within the limits of plausible social-collective effort, the collectivist prefers direct equalization of consumption of specific goods and services.

The individualist and the collectivist are likely to settle for differing social compromises in the world of pervasive inequality. Institutions that overtly and explicitly perpetrate inequalities in endowments and capacities are subject to the individualist's most severe attacks. He will tend to place confiscatory inheritance taxation high on his scale for social reform. He will lend his support to massive public outlays on general education, and he will support selective programs to eliminate poverty. He will tend to oppose an "establishment," and he will oppose the political ambitions of the Kennedys and the Rockefellers. The collectivist will, by comparison, acquiesce in a continuing and pervasive inequality in capacities if he can secure a sufficient measure of consumption equalization. His reform efforts are concentrated on collectivizing activities as a means of securing uniformity. He will tend to advocate a nationally collectivized health service, extensive programs for public housing, public recreation facilities, public libraries, publicly financed cultural programs, publicly operated as well as public-financed education, public television broadcasting.

This summary is not intended to suggest that individuals can be found who fit perfectly into either the individualist or the collectivist mold. Within himself, an individual may be a mixture of the two positions that I have compared. What I am trying to demonstrate is that the manner in which human or personal inequality is interpreted, which is essentially an empirical estimation, may be an important influence on a person's views on social policy. Social scientists have perhaps been too prone to reduce disagreements on policy to value arguments. Ideally considered, the "good society" of the individualist may not be much different from that of the collectivist. Practicably, however, because of the differences in interpretation of inequality, these may remain poles apart.

Evidence and Its Implications

The unrest and dissent that are characteristic of young persons everywhere can be interpreted as a rejection of the collectivist attempts to impose conformity. It would be hard to explain this behavioral revolution by any appeal to endowment or capacity differentials. The shift in attitudes reflects the expression of personal differences in tastes, notably those among groups. The students simply have different preference functions from those of their elders. They choose to live differently.

All of this may be regarded as a refutation of the equal-preferences hypothesis. It cannot be interpreted as corroboration of the equal-capacities hypothesis. If "socialism is dead" as a potentially viable social structure, there is still no sign that individualism can emerge in its stead. The reaction against conformism, against centralization, against bureaucracy—this may possibly result in some limitations on the range of collective control over man's actions. This may provide some opportunity for reforms aimed at reducing inequalities in capacities, and account for the greater emphasis now being placed on selectivity in governmental programs. Even with such policy reforms, however, there is no basis for predicting that any equal-capacities hypothesis will be proved. Facts cannot be made into fable, and we must recognize that, in spite of policy, individuals may differ significantly in inherent personal capacities to create values. Empirically, Plato's hypothesis of inequality may not be refuted, no matter how much we might prefer Adam Smith's. The inequalities that we see may stem from both attributes, and satisfactorily corrective measures may be beyond the scope of social policy.

Where does this leave the social philosopher? A subsidiary theme of this paper is that modern social philosophy, in either its individualist or its collectivist variant, depends critically on one or the other of the equality hypotheses. The ideal world of the individualist contains persons who are basically the same in capacity, and modern democratic and economic institutions in the West were established on the hypothesis that empirical reality can be adjusted to provide a satisfactorily close approximation to that ideal. The ideal world of the socialist contains individuals who are equal in basic tastes, and socialist institutions were established on the hypothesis that empirical reality can be adjusted to reflect this equality despite differing capacities.

What happens when people refuse to accept the distributional inequalities that a practicably ·working capitalist structure requires and at the same time refuse to accept the restrictions on personal freedom that a practicably working collectivism requires? The assorted compromises represented by the mixed social systems of the midtwentieth century may collapse and from differing directions.

I write as an individualist, who yet has little faith in the ultimate corroboration of the equal-capacity hypothesis. From this vantage point, the route toward social stability may involve an increased willingness to tolerate major divergences between our ideals and reality, a recognition that we must proceed "as if" our implied hypothesis were fact, even when we acknowledge that it has little empirical foundation. With Thomas Jefferson, we must sense that in order to treat men "as equals" it may be necessary to tolerate considerable inequality. My counterpart is the collectivist who yet acknowledges that individuals do want different things for themselves. From his vantage point, the route toward greater social stability may involve the more intensive conditioning of individuals to make them accept the conformity that collectivism must impose. In order to secure the distributive equality that he seeks, he must acknowledge that it may be necessary to introduce the inequality in treatment that coercion embodies.

Both the individualist and the collectivist, as I have used these terms here, place positive values on personal freedom and on equality. These basic values may be given different weights and the empirical reading of the world may differ, but neither the individualist nor the collectivist desires to impose his own standards on the rest of society. In this idealized sense, both are democrats; neither is elitist. Within more broadly defined individualist and collectivst categories, however, elitists abound. Many persons propose a smaller public sector primarily because they do not like what is being provided; they should be quite willing to support an enlarged governmental role in society provided only that they could dictate its pattern. Similarly, and perhaps more commonly, many collectivists are dirigistes first and democratic socialists second. They support an extension of state activity because they see in this a means of imposing their own social values on others. The elitist values neither personal freedom nor distributional equality. If either of these values is to be preserved, even at some tolerably acceptable levels of attainment, the nonelitists in both the individualist and the socialist camps may find it necessary to come to some provisional agreement.

14

Public Finance and Academic Freedom

Introduction

I s there an institutional contradiction between the traditional objectives of science and scholarship on the one
hand and public or governmental financial support for
higher learning on the other? Somewhat surprisingly, this
basic question has been neither widely discussed nor critically analyzed. The institutional structure of higher education has mushroomed into its present shape within an
academic heritage that retains trappings of its medieval
forebears. "Academic freedom" historically meant freedom
of the scientist-scholar to inquire and to teach unconstrained
by the shackles of religious dogma. The conjectural history
of Galileo is taken as that of science and scholarship generally. The objective of the continuing struggle is escape
from an all-embracing church. In the medieval world, there
was no independence for the individual, and Galileo's struggle did not find its origins in church subsidization of scholar-

This chapter was initially presented at the Williamsburg Conference of
the Association of Governing Boards of Universities and Colleges in October 1971.

ship. The church did not seek to control his findings because he was a church-financed scholar (indeed he was not), but because these findings were at odds with established dogma. It should not have made one whit of difference whether Galileo was or was not financed from church coffers. The freedom that he sought in Florence, and that has carried over into modern science, was and is freedom from controls by external authority, whether lay or clerical. Can it be explicitly argued that the scholar-scientist properly claims a right to financial support from the same authorities who at the same time are required to grant him his independence? In my view, the origins of academic freedom in any plausibly meaningful sense rest in the absence of constraints on the independent inquiry of the academician, on his freedom to pursue truth where it may lead. It would represent a distortion of history to find in these origins a scholar's claim to sustenance by the institutions whose value structure he explicitly rejects.

The Modern Question

In West and East, scientific inquiry, or, more generally, higher learning, is now predominantly supported by public or governmental authorities. Academic freedom from traditional theological dogma is of no consequence in the West, but the struggles of the scholar in the communist-dominated East remain in most respects comparable to those of Galileo. In the West, by contrast, there are no dogmas to be protected as such, and any realistic assessment must acknowledge the freedom of the independent scientist-scholar to do just about as he pleases, where he pleases, and when he pleases. Hence, we find advocates of astrology, flat earth, and the single tax. The problem in the West is quite a different one. It concerns the intellectual independence of the scientist-scholar-teacher who is not himself independent of support and sustenance by governmental bodies. Does the body politic, the social group as a whole, have some implied obligation to finance the scientist-scholar while allowing him free reign? If so, are there no limits beyond which support becomes questionable in value?

I was provoked into analyzing this set of questions by some of the responses to the little book that I coauthored with Nicos Devletoglou in 1969, *Academia in Anarchy*.[1] Several reviewers of this book, presumably in all seriousness, questioned one of our central premises to the effect that public or governmental financing of higher education necessarily implies public or governmental control, to some degree. We had advanced this proposition in the predictive or positive sense, but we did not question the normative version. As I recall, however, one reviewer stated that the legitimacy of public control as a consequence of public financing was a "highly debatable question." The reviewer in the *Western Political Quarterly*[2] said, "It[the book] disposes glibly of a touchy, controversial issue in suggesting that the taxpayers and donors should control."[3] Until I read such reviews as this, at least in my own thinking, there had been no question at all. The proposition seemed to me cut and dried. This perhaps partially explained my emotional shock when I first observed the antics of the UCLA faculty

---

[1] James M. Buchanan and Nicos Devletoglou, *Academia in Anarchy* (New York: Basic Books, 1970); English edition, 1971.
[2] C. Easton Rothwell, review of *Academia in Anarchy*, in *Western Political Quarterly* 24, no. 1 (March 1971): 212–13.
[3] *Ibid.*, p. 213.

senate during my tenure at that university in 1968–69. I felt as though I had landed in a lunatic asylum, for what I saw were serious and quite famous scholars acting and talking as if the taxpayers of California, acting through Governor Reagan and the board of regents, had some sacred obligation to throw increasing amounts of revenues over the university's ivied walls without so much as a right to inquire what went on behind those walls. The mere slowing up of the rate of increase of this flow of funds, in appropriations of public funds to the university, was sufficient to raise charges of a vicious and unholy attack on academic freedom. And when the board of regents went a step further in the Angela Davis case, when it actually tried to exercise some control over the appointment of an avowed revolutionary to the university faculty, this was taken as a violation of the most sacrosanct of academia's domains.

My own prejudices on these matters are, I am sure, clear from the tone of my remarks. But there are matters of substance apart from prejudice or emotion to be discussed here. Is there a case to be made for public financing of higher education *without* public control?

The Implications of Public Financing

First of all, we must be clear about just what public or governmental financing is. Whether the funds are derived from federal, state, or local governmental sources, whether these funds are in the form of explicit appropriations or of tax-exempt contributions, the ultimate source is tax revenues. And taxes are compulsory exactions from citizens of the appropriate jurisdiction. To introduce legitmacy here, it must be possible somehow to derive a conceptual logic through which individual citizens, as taxpayers, can be shown to enjoy specific benefits from the utilization of tax revenues in this or that way, and benefits in excess of those which might be expected to be forthcoming upon alternative public or private uses of the same funds. And, of course, ultimately the test of the existence of such benefits lies in the continued expressed willingness of the taxpayers, acting through their political representatives, to support the outlays that are under consideration. Note particularly that we must talk about the general taxpayer's calculus of benefits here, and not about the family whose children are eligible for subsidized education. The benefits to the latter are no different from those received from the enjoyment of any other good or service, be this bread or gasoline, and there is no argument under the sun which can be called upon to justify governmental subsidization of what amounts to essentially private consumption of educational services. To derive any justification at all for governmental financial support from taxes compulsorily levied on all citizens, we must be able to show, at least conceptually, just what *general* benefits the taxpayer who secures no purely private consumption benefits receives from the outlays to higher educational institutions.

Once we so much as approach the issue in this way, we may begin to put some handles on an otherwise mushy discussion. Just what benefit can the average taxpayer expect to get from throwing his money over the ivy wall especially if the scholars presumably at work behind this wall are to be allowed complete freedom to expend this money as they see fit. Once the question is put in this way, it is those who try to defend freedom of the academy from external political controls who are put on the defensive. They must produce positive answers which indicate the intrinsic value inherent in "academic freedom" so defined. It is no longer legitimate for these bleeding academicians to require public or governmental authorities to make out a case for interfering in the sacred groves. For unless the taxpayers' questions can be answered satisfactorily, the ultimate effective control is necessarily present and it will be exercised through the simple withdrawal of funds. The greatest fools in the modern world are found in the academy; we all know this, but even among these it is hard to think of anyone so much a fool as to think that the taxpayers would blindly finance bomb factories, if things should come to such a pass.

I have personally been surprised at the extreme reluctance of governmental authorities, who act presumably in the interests of taxpayers in some indirect way, to take more steps toward control both through budgetary restrictions and otherwise. I recognize that there are time lags between recognition and action, and between action and effect, and I also recognize the political power of the entrenched educational bureaucracy at all governmental levels, but even when all of these are taken into account, I should have predicted that, after the campus disruptions of the 1960s, we would have experienced a much more severe academic recession than we have observed in the 1970s.

What does the general taxpayer get when he supports the institutions of higher learning? Does he get, or can he expect to get, value for money, as my English friends would say? In the private market economy, the buyer gets value for his money because of his ability to shop around among alternative sellers. In ordinary governmental services, the taxpayer may not be able to shop around, but his representatives exercise tight controls by specifying in advance just what it is they are paying for. A road improvement, a new firehouse, an extra garbage pickup per week—these are quite specific, and there is relatively little uncertainty about the final results to be expected. The problem with education, and notably with higher education, is the extreme uncertainty about just what the final product is. What is the output that the general taxpayer expects to get for his taxes?

We may be more specific and ask the question: What should the general taxpayer in, say, Virginia or South Carolina expect to secure if the political decision-structure increased the annual rate of outlay to higher education by $10 million? In quantity terms, a large number of persons could be provided with college or university instruction; in quality terms, a "better" and more intensive program could be provided. Emphasis on the research side of higher education could be increased. These are, of course, the familiar and standard answers, and it is perhaps fortunate for those of us who earn our bread in higher education that most people remain satisfied by this level of response. If we look at these answers critically, however, their emptiness is apparent. What are the benefits from having a larger number of persons put through the nonspecified higher educational process, and what are the benefits from a "better" program if the criteria for "better" and "worse" are unknown to all save the insiders?

The Mythology of Higher Education

Every age has its mythology, and the mythological role occupied by higher education in the modern world should not be underestimated. To the general taxpayer or to the private donor, the provision of financial support for higher

education is a form of expiation before his gods. It is un-
realistic to deny this as fact, and one that college and university administrators recognize far better than many of
their faculty colleagues. In this image, of course, the mysteries of higher education are part of its attraction, and
exposure involves predictable disaffection. In this respect,
modern institutions of higher learning can yet look to the
successful churches of all ages. The priest holds the awe of
the masses only so long as he remains within the temple,
only so long as he stays above the crowd, only so long as he
speaks to the gods. Once he sallies forth among the rabble,
he is seen for the man that he is, his robes for the simple
cloth it is, and his voice heard as but one among a multitude.

The quantum leap in higher education that we have experienced in the quarter-century since World War II was
supported by this mystique. Parents who themselves had
not shared the mysteries remained in awe of academe. The
history of higher education in the next quarter-century must
be quite different. Parents have seen the inner workings of
the temple. This exposure was accompanied by the politicization of the late 1960s. The high priests as well as their
acolytes soiled their garments by entering into affairs of the
world, where their performance could be, and was, judged
by ordinary men on their own standards. And who can
claim that, empirically, the image of higher education was
enhanced in the process?

If the public is to be convinced that it should continue to
support higher education through the 1970s and the 1980s,
on a scale comparable to the relative support of past decades, without imposing controls over the output, something
beyond the mythology must be invoked. Exposure has dis-
pelled the myth, although elements of this remain and some

restoration is always possible. But myths are notoriously vulnerable precisely because they are myths. We should at least hope that there is something more of substance that can be introduced to justify general public support independent of explicit public control, and exercised as such.

Professional Training

First, we must say something about purely professional training, largely to get this out of the way in our discussion. In professional training, the uncertainties about just what the product is are largely absent, and control is exercised directly or indirectly to ensure that the desired quality product is forthcoming. The medical school faculty is severely limited in its freedom of action by the standards imposed, with public sanction, by the medical associations. How many professors of acupuncture are found in the accredited medical schools, and this is a far more respectable approach to medical care than many of the other approaches that full "academic freedom" might produce if medical faculties were allowed absolutely free reign.

Whether or not there is a legitimate economic argument for tax support of purely professional training is quite another question that I need not go into in this paper. To the extent that the skills acquired enhance the direct earnings potential of those who are trained, there seems no basis for general taxpayer support. But this opens up a topic that is not directly relevant to my main argument. The point I emphasize here is that, because the product is known, the purely professional training aspects of the modern university or college are rather closely controlled to ensure that the desired product is in fact produced.

The problem that I address here is concentrated on the nonprofessional aspects of higher education.

The Hard Sciences

It is best to consider the various aspects of college-university education in ascending order of difficulty. Professional training has been discussed. The genuinely hard sciences occupy a halfway position. There are genuine social benefits which result from scientific discovery, benefits which accrue to all persons in society and which cannot readily be captured by individuals. And as Michael Polanyi has so eloquently argued, discovery cannot be externally controlled or planned, precisely because it is discovery. Polanyi's analogy is that of the unfinished jigsaw puzzle, with only a few parts complete, and with the more comprehensive picture remaining unrecognizable. The progress toward solution can best be advanced by allowing separate scholars to work independently with the jumble of pieces, having complete freedom in their never-ending search for patterns. Science ventures into the unknown, and produces results that benefit us all. Within some limits, there is a legitimate basis, therefore, for governmental support for the activity of scientific discovery, for the subsidization of science and the training of future scientists, and *without* specific definition of the end product or result that is expected to be forthcoming, and *without* overt external control over the activity of discovery itself. [The limits here are those which are required to prevent scientific inquiry from going off into purely esoteric and wholly remote areas of research.]

Even here, however, an important proviso must be

added. The "academic freedom" of the college-university scientist to seek truth where he finds it and to report his discoveries openly, and to train future scientists as he sees fit—this freedom can be stoutly defended, even when the scientist secures his sustenance from governmental authorities. The proviso here is and must be the willingness of the scientist to remain within the boundaries of science as such. The academic freedom of the mathematician scarcely extends to his "right" to convert his classroom into a laboratory for revolution. The governmental authorities who finance his efforts have an obligation to ensure that the practicing teacher-scientist-scholar stays within the appropriate limits. And it is a perversion of the whole concept of academic freedom to interpret it as extending to the prohibition of such attempts at external control.

Under normal circumstances, and historically, the exercise of external controls to this purpose have very rarely been necessary. Practicing scientists in college and university communities could be relied on to adhere to the common standards of behavior that academic life embodied. But we do not live in normal times, and the academia of today is not a simple linear extension of that which has gone before. Can we now depend on all of those who hold college or university appointments to stay within the bounds that warrant or justify their own freedom? I raise this as a question; you can provide your own answers. Or, if you are a member of the academic community itself, the question may be turned around. Should we not take steps, internally, to ensure that our scientists, those who do deserve to be left alone, will, in fact, be left alone? This involves, not the blind and unthinking defense of the academia against any and all external attempts at control, but, instead, the correc-

What Should Economists Do?

tion of internal abuses that we all recognize to exist. Those so-called scientists among us who overtly flaunt academic freedom by allowing their classrooms and laboratories to become politicized should be eliminated from our ranks.

The Liberal Arts

Any justification of public or governmental support without public or governmental control becomes much more difficult when we shift from the hard sciences to the soft sciences, the arts, the humanities—all of which we conveniently summarize under the "liberal arts" rubric. What benefits can the general taxpayer, the man who is subjected to involuntary fiscal contributions, properly or legitimately expect from a system that educates more young persons in the "liberal arts," or which educates them "better," or which does both? What demonstrable improvements in the level or the quality of life are to be predicted as a result of this public investment of funds?

Clearly we have entered upon a stage of discourse quite different from that which is relevant for the hard sciences. There is little role for "discovery" as such, and indeed one of the acknowledged fallacies of all ages is the facile extension of "scientific" solutions to social, intellectual, philosophical, and cultural issues. We should not expect an improved technology from higher learning in the liberal arts. Another way of stating this is to say that education here involves the search for essentially the same eternal verities that have been discussed since the early Greeks. What we expect to get from higher education is not an improvement in the standards of living for unchanged men— which improvement does summarize the objectives of both the hard sciences and the professions—but the converse. From higher education in the liberal arts we expect to get *changed men whose own standards or objectives for life are themselves "better" or of "higher quality."*

"The making of higher-quality men"—this familiar high-sounding objective has an appealing and persuasive ring. But we sense the emptiness once we think at all critically about definitions of quality. Who is to judge? By whose criteria are qualities to be determined? And here is seems to me self-evident that the ultimate judges will be, and should be, the members of the general public itself, the source of the funds for the social investment that publicly financed higher education represents. This is not to say that the general public, acting as required through political representatives, defines quality by its own self-image. Quite the contrary. Higher education is expected to turn out "better" men. There are accepted standards of "betterness" to which each one of us aspires but which remain unachieved, and all of us can point to other men who outrank us on our own scales. Similarly, there are the accompanying criteria of "worseness"; these we seek to avoid but sometimes fail, and all of us can point to other men who are "worse" by our own standards of evaluation.

Academia and the Standards of Society

These are trite, but necessary, observations for the point I am trying to develop here. The "product" of our higher educational institutions is constantly being evaluated by the prevailing value standards of the society. So long as the objectives are fulfilled, the details of the "production" process need not be, and indeed should not be, of concern to the ultimate purchaser, in this case, the public at large. So long as our colleges and universities, the users of tax funds, are observed to produce young persons who are demonstrably "better" than their noneducated cohorts by prevailing social standards, there need be no external interference with the inner workings of the institutions. Academic freedom can be honored in the observance, and liberal scholars-teachers can be allowed to pursue their own purposes without constraints imposed by the political authorities who hold the purse strings. (Of course, political authorities have not always recognized the principles outlined here, and unjustifiable interferences with academic freedom have occurred.)

The situation today may, however, be something that is quite different from that which has been experienced, at least in this country. Un the 1960s, at least, or so it seems to me, the publicly supported institutions of higher learning did meet the general objectives noted. But I question their status at present. If you will allow me, for a moment, to strip off my academic regalia and express myself solely and exclusively as a member of the general taxpaying public, I should argue that the "product" now issuing from many of our tax-supported liberal arts colleges and universities does not measure up to my standards of human quality improvement. Instead of turning out "better" men and women, some of these institutions seem to me to be producing at least some young men and women who are demonstrably "worse" than their counterparts who did not enjoy the benefits of my tax dollars. I have on several occasions, along with others, called some of these products the "new barbarians," a term which seems descriptive in several respects and for which I find no need to apologize.

The Status of Academic Freedom

It is here that an emergent clash between "academic freedom," as this is defined by the scholars behind the ivied walls, and "public finance" seems almost unavoidable. If the tax-supported institutions of higher learning are not fulfilling the objectives for which they are presumably funded, the general public, through its political authorities, fails in its task if it does not act. Either of two courses of action is open. Financial support can be withdrawn. This allows the precepts of academic freedom to be strictly observed, and the financially debilitated colleges and universities that survive can be allowed the freedom to espouse dogmas as their faculties desire. But this amounts to an abandonment of the whole social objective of publicly supported higher education and an admission that a glorious experiment has failed and dismally. The alternative course of action must involve an attempt by the public to exercise minimal controls on the educational processes, controls designed to ensure that the objectives of the social investment are not perverted.

If this action is chosen, it will necessarily embody an invasion of academic freedom, as this is defined by most of the left-liberals who dominate today's academic faculties. But if the nation's tax-supported colleges and universities (including those supported indirectly through tax deductions) are producing outputs that do not measure up to expectations, should we not anticipate this rational response? Perhaps academicians have become too spoiled to recognize that the institutions of higher learning will not be allowed to continue their existence as free-floating islands whose only connection with the public is financial support, and whose drift is dictated by the fashions of modern intellectuals.

I should not attempt to predict the precise form that external controls will take, and I should emphasize that I am not saying here that all of our institutions of higher learning, in whole or in part, have necessarily failed in their social responsibility. Even the "worst" institutions succeed in producing young men and women whose quality genuinely represents demonstrable and substantial returns on the social investment that their training embodies. And the "best" institutions, those which did not acquiesce in the debasements of the 1960s, may still be producing critically informed and tolerant youngsters who are "better" than their forebears, and who are recognized as such by the body politic. Unfortunately, however, the general public does not, and cannot, fully discriminate in its evaluative judgments. The public views the excrescence of the higher educational output, and it does not like what it sees. It will not, for long, be satisfied with mere pronouncements that those who are most evident represent only a tiny activist minority of students, especially in the wake of burned-out buildings, broken windows, and widespread behavioral pollution.

It would, of course, be proper, as well as helpful, to say that, recognizing all of this, the academic houses should put themselves in order, that the faculties of our colleges and universities should from within implement reforms which will turn things around. This may occur; all things are possible. But I have personally lost faith in the ability of faculties to initiate and carry through internal reforms. To accomplish this, faculties would have to be everywhere exercising greater selectivity and discrimination in decisions on appointment, promotion, and tenure. More important, we should also observe faculties taking active steps to weed out those from among their own ranks who have openly and explicitly broken the trust that binds men in communities of scholarship and science, those who have chosen to politicize critical scholarship, those who have moved the modern university out of its traditional role and into avowed adherence of values not countenanced in the society at large.

Unfortunately, what we do observe is almost the opposite. Instead of trying to preserve academic freedom for us all by putting things aright internally, faculties tend to spring to the defense of those of their own ranks who have been responsible for the public reaction. In this, faculties invite the very controls from outside that they presumably abhor.

As the political authorities attempt to exercise control over the inner workings of the institutions of academia, they are doomed to frustration and at least partial failure. Just as its criticism is undiscriminating, so must be the general public's interferences. Attempted controls may worsen rather than improve matters, and the programs that are most deserving of public support may suffer more than those deserving censure because of the workings of the academic bureaucracies. This result may, in its turn, alienate those from among the faculties who have recognized the need for reforms. Through such a process, colleges and universities everywhere may be shifted more and more into the Latin American pattern. They may increasingly become isolated centers of revolutionary or quasi-revolutionary activity that are allowed to exist but that are increasingly drained of financial support from society generally.

This is not a happy picture of academia in the late 1970s or in 1984. But I should tell you that I am by nature a pessimist, and I acknowledge that some of the predictions about academia that I made in 1969 have proven false. The 1970s have not matched the insanities of the 1960s. The slight but perceptible academic recession that did occur worked wonders in toning down the arrogance of the professional elite, both existing and emerging. The mystique of higher education may be strong enough to carry us through the bas patch, and academia in the 1980s may shine with newfound glory. It would be nice to be able to end on this note, but honesty compels me to introduce the required qualifications. I see nothing in the wind that suggests a return to reason, the retreat from which has gone on apace since the mid-1960s. I see nothing that indicates the end of the new age of romantic nonsense that characterizes modern intellectual discourse. I see no signs of increasing critical awareness along with a return to tolerance and, yes, to elementary good manners.

In academia and elsewhere, the retreat goes on from social philosophy in its positive sense, and the reality of the genuinely free and open society seems more distant than ever. Because of an absence of elementary courage in our makeup at all decision levels, we become increasingly vulnerable to exploitation. We need, and need desperately, to recover the social faith and intellectual courage that were America's. If modern intellectuals, in our universities and outside, should begin to worry more about meeting this challenge and less about the defense of some meretricious academic freedom, there would indeed be grounds for hope.

15

Public Choice and Ideology

It is impossible to deny that *public choice* has embodied a "theory of government failure" that is on all fours with the "theory of market failure" embodied in theoretical welfare economics. In saying this, I am *not* saying that public choice implies government failure *relative* to market alternatives. I am saying that relative to the images of government prevalent in the 1940s, public choice has embodied a theory of government failure. Public choice, along with complementary empirical observation, has defused enthusiasm for collectivist solutions to social problems. In this negative sense, public choice has exerted, and continues to exert, major ideological impact.

Public choice has also been important in opening up for inspection and evaluation previously sacrosanct aspects of social interaction. In so doing, it has become more difficult for intellectually self-respecting scholars to maintain mutually inconsistent standards for the evaluation of separate organizational alternatives. The economist who analyzes the distance between the market order that he observes and

This chapter was initially prepared for presentation in a panel discussion at the Public Choice Society meeting, New Orleans, March 1978.

that which satisfies his formalized conditions for optimality cannot, by neglect, imply preference for the collectivist alternative. He can no longer act like the judge who awarded the prize to the second singer after he had heard the first. I am not here saying that my colleagues in economics have quit doing this. I am saying only that exposure to public choice makes it more difficult for them to do so.

It seems extremely difficult for anyone to adopt a socialist position and at the same time be familiar with and accept the analysis of public choice. Here I use *socialist* in the sense that this term was employed in the 1930s, when Lange, Lerner, and others convinced so many of their colleagues that socialism could *work*. No more than a smattering of sophistication in public choice (or in ordinary common sense, for that matter) is required to suggest the absurdity in that position. Once any thought at all is given to the actual processes of collective decision-making, the claims for efficiency-generating properties of the socialist alternative collapse of their own weight.

Admittedly, my comment here applies to what has been called "market socialism," or, more generally, to what is still occasionally called "democratic socialism." The authoritarian socialist position is immensely stronger in terms of logical consistency. Democratic decisions cannot run a society, but perhaps the experts, the technocrats, the social engineers, the planners, can do so. What is there in public-choice theory that also gives the lie to the planning advocates? We need only return to the ancient Roman query: Who is to guard the guardians? Planners are also utility-maximizing individuals, and who could predict that planning decisions will be made contrary to the interests of those who make them?

Let me now shift beyond the ideological positions that might, in one sense, be classified as "economic," and examine the position I have sometimes called the "transcendentalist." In this position, politics is an activity that seeks "truth," and political process is a means of arriving at "truth judgments." There exist objectively defined "true" solutions to all political questions, and the task of politics and political scholars is to find them. This position captures the essence of classical political theory. It must be apparent that such a stance rejects the central organizing hypothesis of public choice, namely, the derivation of collective outcomes from the utility-maximizing behavior of individuals. Implicit in public-choice analysis is the notion that only individuals have values or preferences, that there are really no transcendent truths to be discovered by some mysterious process of political discourse. There are relatively few Straussians among us.

Let me move along in my array of philosophical positions or ideological stances that seem inconsistent with public-choice theory. We can, I think, dismiss the anarchist position readily, whether this be the romantic or the libertarian variety. Public-choice theory deals with persons as utility-maximizing beings, not as disembodied spirits full of love, or even as mindful of each other's "natural boundaries."

This leaves me with the Marxist position, which requires discussion at somewhat greater length. In some of his explanation of observed politics, the Marxist is closer to the public-choice theorist than either of them is to the "public-interest" theory of politics. Where the Marxist conception departs from the public-choice conception is in its failure to construct its analysis within an individualistic frame of reference. Persons cannot be rational utility maximizers and at the same time behave so as to further the interests of the social class in which they are located or to which they have arbitrarily assigned themselves. To say that class position dominates and drives behavior is fully analogous to saying that a person behaves always to further the public interest. After all, all of the members of the community are a "class." One model seems as empty of content as the other. Or as full.

So much for an array of those philosophical positions or ideologies that seem to be inconsistent with a considered internalization of the principles of public-choice theory. Let me turn briefly to consider those positions that seem broadly consistent. I group these into two sets, which I label the Panglossian and the meliorist. By Panglossian I refer to those views that imply, directly or indirectly, that there is really nothing that can be done to improve matters; hence, we live in the best of possible worlds. I am not quite sure that we can properly label these positions as "ideologies," but you will recognize them.

First, there is the pure Hobbesian, who asserts that everyone prefers order to anarchy and that only the sovereign can secure order. But there is no control over the passions of the sovereign. Relax and enjoy, if you can. My point here is only that this basic Hobbesian world view is compatible with public choice. All persons are utility maximizers. Much the same can be said for the Paretian world view, which is closely related to the Hobbesian. There always exists a sharp delineation between the rulers, the elite few, and the ruled. The elites may circulate, but there is no mythology of democratic control. Rulers rule in their own interest, and the ruled try to evade the rules to the extent that self-interest dictates. The task of the social scientist is to observe the uniformities, to identify the residues.

I should also put into the Panglossian category what I have defined as the social evolutionist position, which I associate with Oakeshott and Hayek. Efficient institutions tend to emerge through a spontaneous process of decentralized adjustment, akin to the common law, and attempts to design, lay on, or construct improvements must be self-defeating. I mention this philosophical perspective only to note that it is not, *per se,* inconsistent with the principles that drive the theory of public choice.

So much for the Panglossian varieties. Each of the world views described is broadly consistent with public choice because each can embody the presumption that individuals are rational utility maximizers in all capacities and roles.

Let me now turn very briefly to the meliorist position or ideology that is consistent with the principles of public choice, and you will not be surprised to learn that this is my own position. I refer, of course, to the constitutionalist-contractarian position, which is based in the recognition that individuals are utility maximizing and rational, and that they recognize that they are. Hence, there will be the need for "constitutions," for "rules," to constrain the behavior of persons, privately and collectively, and public choice offers the normative understanding necessary to lay down "better" rules. The Hobbesian scenario is rejected empirically; we observe that governments have been limited by constitutional constraints. We also reject the evolutionist view; we have observed designed or constructed social arrangements that work.

I have tried to suggest that certain positions are consist-

ent with public choice while others are not. I am not implying in making this classification that everyone who works
in public choice has a well-defined philosophical position.
Many scholars do not. These scholars proceed in what they
conceive to be their roles as "scientists," discovering many
old wheels and a few new ones, with relatively little concern for the implications of "scientific findings" for a normative understanding of social order. To the extent that these
social "scientists" among us really think that the problems
of living together in organized community lend themselves
to scientific solution, I think they are seriously deluded. But
to discuss this point in detail would be both to repeat what
many others have said and to go on far too long.

Part Four

Postscript

16

Retrospect and Prospect

One of Professor Hayek's most renowned essays is titled "Why I Am Not a Conservative." I am tempted to emulate Hayek here and entitle this postscript essay, "Why I Am Not an Economist." To anyone who reads the methodological urgings contained in the essays of this volume, written over almost two decades, and who simultaneously looks at what passes for "economics" in the professional journals of 1980, there is only one evident conclusion. The author of the essays is almost the only one in step or else he writes under some delusion that he is something that he is not.

If not an economist, what am I? An outdated freak whose functional role in the general scheme of things has passed into history? Perhaps I should accept such an assessment, retire gracefully, and, with alcoholic breath, hoe my cabbages. Perhaps I could do so if the modern technicians had indeed produced "better" economic mousetraps. Instead of evidence of progress, however, I see a continuing erosion of the intellectual (and social) capital that was accumulated by "political economy" in its finest hours. I look at young colleagues trained to master regression routines who are totally uninterested in, and incompetent to examine, elementary economic propositions. The graduate schools attract and turn out dullards, and the exciting young minds turn increasingly to law, to philosophy, and to the commune. For those among these minds that are trapped into economics and that may, with effort, partially finesse the empiricist rage, I see them compelled to utilize their considerable mental potentials resolving the escapist puzzles of modern mathematics.

It is precisely because the discipline of economics, as practiced, seems so bad and to be getting worse, that I find continued interest and challenge in pursuing what some might think a hopeless cause. But Frank Knight comes to my rescue here as elsewhere when I recall his equation— to call a situation hopeless is the same as to call it ideal. Ideal things are not. And with hope for improvement, fun remains in the game.

In this postscript essay, my best procedure would seem to be to take stock and to reiterate, I hope with variety, some of the central themes developed in the earlier pieces, and, in particular, to suggest possible directions that seem ripe for further inquiry. I propose to do this through a series of cryptic statements or assertions, each one of which is followed by only a brief explanatory discussion. My purpose is to challenge thought, not to convince by argument.

1. *Economics is a very peculiar "science."* As previously noted, there is a "science" of economics, but it bears little or no similarity to the physical-biological sciences, as the latter are normally conceived. Economics is "predictive" in a totally different sense, and the indirect implications for "control" are not comparable. The problems in economics are not amenable to scientific solutions, and progress is not to be expected by pushing back the frontiers of science. The

strictures of both Frank Knight and F. A. Hayek against scientism require continued repetition.

2. *Economics is about choice.* If economics were scientific in the strict predictive sense, it could not be concerned with choice at all, as G. L. S. Shackle should have taught us all. Choice is necessarily made among imagined "possibles," and choice-making under certainty becomes internally contradictory. The equilibrium constructions are useful only if their limitations are appreciated. These allow us to discuss directions of adjustment rather than states of potential attainability.

3. *Economics involves actors.* Without actors, there is no play. This truism has been overlooked by modern economists whose universe is peopled with passive responders to stimuli. If all are price-takers, who sets price? If all behavior is rationally responsive, how can change occur? How can entrepreneurship be modeled? Increasingly, I have come to the view that the role of entrepreneurship has been the most neglected area of economic inquiry, with significant normative implications for the general understanding of how the whole economy works.

4. *Economics is about arbitrage.* The behavioral paradigm central to economics is that of the trader whose Smithean propensity to truck and barter locates and creates opportunities for mutual gains. This paradigm is contrasted with that of the maximizing engineer who allocates scarce resources among alternatives. As several of the essays in this volume have suggested, the maximization paradigm is the fatal methodological flaw in modern economics.

5. *Economics is about a game within rules.* Choices are made by actors, by traders, constrained within specifically

determined "laws and institutions," a central emphasis of Adam Smith and one that has been lost to modern minds. Institutions matter. The libertarian anarchists who dream of markets without states are romantic fools, who have read neither Hobbes nor history.

6. *Economics is political.* Choices are also made among rules and sets of rules. The "social contract" also offers mutuality of gains, and indeed, the "social miracle" must remain central to man's consciousness. Passive acquiescence in the developing events of history, by scholars and non-scholars, must produce the natural reversion to the jungle.

7. *Economics has a didactic role.* As a discipline or area of inquiry, economics has social value in offering an understanding of the principle of order emergent from decentralized processes, of spontaneous coordination. (The market is the classic example.) Such an understanding is necessarily prior to an informed decision on alternative forms of social order, or even on alternative directions of marginal extension. The principle of order that economics teaches is in no way "natural" to the human mind which, in innocence, is biased toward simplistic collectivism.

8. *Economics is elementary.* Finally, and despite the attempts by modern scholars to cloak their own insecurity in complexity, the central principles of economics are elementary. We do not need the excess baggage of modern mathematics to grasp and to convey the basic wisdom that Adam Smith discovered and that his successors emphasized.

So much for a cryptic but serious listing of my own ABCs of economic method, circa 1980. In one way or another, each of the statements finds a reasoned defense in one or more of the main essays in this book.

I stated earlier that there is hope for improvement in economics, despite the downhill slide that I attributed to the discipline. Let me end this postscript by noting a few encouraging signs. Theorists are asking who sets prices. Theorists are beginning to evaluate alternative institutional structures. Economists are increasingly coming to accept the notion that law and the structure of rights can have consequences. Work proceeds apace on the analysis and evaluation of governmental structures. Any public-sector, private-sector decision made in 1980 must be much better informed than one made in, say, 1960. Entrepreneurship is on the verge of becoming something again worthy of economists' attention. The false objectivity of choice alternatives is beginning to look very frayed around the edges. Subjectivist economics has become respectable after a long time in the wilderness. The analysis of choices among rules, as contrasted to choices within rules, has come to command increasing attention, not only in the constitutional-postconstitutional distinctions in public choice and in Rawlsian political philosophy, but also in the newer examination of individual self-control. Attention is being paid to the relevance and importance of economic perception.

As I list these hopeful signs of change, of stirrings in the discipline, broadly defined, I may seem to contradict my earlier diagnosis of doom and gloom. This reading is valid only in part. The signs of constructive change that I have listed immediately above are outside the mainstream interests of the profession, and they will likely remain so for at least a decade. Nonetheless, I keep the faith, and there is some prospect that the economics of 2000 will be judged better than that of 1980, and by my standards.

Index

This book was set in Times Roman. The face was designed by Stanley Morison to be used in the news columns of the London *Times*. The *Times* was seeking a typeface that would be condensed enough to accommodate a substantial number of words per column without sacrificing readability and still have an attractive, contemporary appearance. The design was an immediate success. It is used in many periodicals throughout the world and is one of the most popular text faces currently in use for book work.

Jacket, hardcover case, and cover design by Erin Kirk New,
    Watkinsville, Georgia
Book design by Design Center, Inc., Indianapolis, Indiana
Typography by Weimer Typesetting Co., Inc., Indianapolis, Indiana